SECRETS

OF BECOMING A

PRIORITY PATIENT

Keys To Becoming An 'Insider' In The Health Care System

Dr. Ronald S. Baigrie

and

Colleen McKinnon

Published by The Medical School For Patients

362.1
BAI

National Library of Canada Cataloguing In Publication

Baigrie, Ronald S.
  Secrets of becoming a priority patient : keys to becoming an insider in the health care system / Ronald S. Baigrie, Colleen McKinnon.

ISBN 0-9732226-0-3

  1. Patient participation. 2. Patient satisfaction. I. McKinnon, Colleen, 1972- II. Title.

R727.42.B33 2003   362.1   C2003-902000-2

Published By:
The Medical School For Patients
Sudbury, Ontario
P3E 1B8

Cover Design By:
50 Carleton & Associates
Sudbury, Ontario

Printed in Canada By:
Central Printers
Sudbury, Ontario

Portrait By:
Alfred Boyd Studios
Sudbury, Ontario

Illustrations By:
Vincenzo Franco - Visual Works
Sudbury, Ontario

Copying Information

We encourage limited reproduction of any part of this book (up to 20 pages) without express permission from the author as long as the title of the book and name of the author remain on the copy. Please clearly explain to others where you discovered the ideas presented in this book and where you purchased your copy. The purpose of any form of reproduction should respect the intent of this publication; patient education.

Regarding Gender

With respect to the issue of gender, we have chosen to assume (for the purpose of simplicity) that the doctor in this book is a 58-year-old male. It was brought to our attention that alternating the age and gender of our doctor was confusing for the reader. Our patient where applicable is female.

Regarding Partnerships

With respect to the issue of patient/physician partnership, we recognise that some patients will prefer to seek out and create a long-term relationship with an individual physician who will advise them on their health care needs. Many other patients will prefer to form a patient/system partnership. They will utilize the strategies and principles contained in this book when interacting with each of the medical professionals they encounter when accessing the health care system. Your choice will reflect your approach to life. Good luck!

Acknowledgments

Many friends and colleagues contributed to the publication of this book.
With special thanks to the following:

Diane Kirkpatrick
Maureen Mills
Tina Emley
Mary-Liz Warwick
Jim Young
Bill Cook
Cal McDonald
Gord White
Tom Kirkpatrick
Real Fortin
Henry Goegan
Linda Ryan
Chris Gavard

The proceeds from the sale of this book will be directed to further development of The Medical School For Patients.

To all those patients who have allowed me to enter into their lives and participate in a very personal process, you have taught me that a doctor should not only be a scientist, but a partner, a friend and a confidant.

Thank You

Table of Contents

III. HOSPITALS AND YOU

IV. KNOWLEDGE AND YOU

V. SAFETY AND YOU

EPILOGUE

Attention...

*Just prior to the first printing of this book, a document titled "**Building A Safer System**" was released by the National Steering Committee on Patient Safety. This report, representing a national strategy to improve patient safety, was sponsored by the Royal College of Physicians and Surgeons of Canada with input from over 50 leaders representing government, health care associations and many other non-government organizations. A few notable recommendations are:*

*.... "Health-care personnel, patients and all others within the system must be **informed participants** in understanding that human error is inevitable and that underlying systemic factors, including ongoing system change contribute to most near misses, adverse events and critical incidents"...*

*.... "Develop educational materials on **personal measures** for improving safety in health-care for distribution to the public"...*

*.... "The health-care system must encourage partnerships among all consumers and providers of care. **Partnerships** will require the health-care system to become more flexible, with a shift away from traditional hierarchical operating structures. These partnerships, including those of individuals, professions and organizations, are necessary for effectively improving all operational/systemic deficiencies"...*

*.... "Develop and implement responsive **patient-focused** programs for the receipt, review and management of concerns within health-care organizations"...*

In our opinion, the advice and guidance offered in this book is in agreement with the philosophy advocated in this report. Perhaps the only point of departure is our emphasis on the Priority Patient as the major driving force to ensure that health-care is ultimately individualized.

PREFACE

I love what I do. I'm a doctor; a Cardiologist graduated in 1969 from the University of Toronto. You don't realize it, but you are about to read a one of a kind book. In it you will find some provocative sections which will stimulate you to think and others which may cause you some concern. I firmly believe that every patient must take control of their health. Each patient should understand and manage their symptoms and diseases in a partnership arrangement with their doctors.

There are more choices to be made in medicine today than ever before. Patients should be aware of the many possible options in diagnosis and therapy. By understanding these options they can choose those most appropriate to their own very personal situation. Patients should participate as equal partners in decision making. They should not simply surrender this fundamental component of health care to the whim of their physician. If they fully understand the rationale for choosing particular treatment strategies, they can better appreciate the possible outcomes. Doctors who know their patients well automatically taper treatment strategies to each individual patient. Others may not. A physician's preference may not always be the patient's first choice or indeed be in the patient's best interest!

I have found that ignorance and misinformation can be more disabling than disease itself. Today, there are many more patients with long-term illness. These patients require ongoing advice on how to live with their disease. This can only be accomplished with individual education and active participation. There are many professionals available to offer advice and expert opinion. However, all health care workers have personal built-in biases demonstrated by preferences for managing diseases in particular ways. Patients need to evaluate this advice and ensure that it reflects their individuality. Remember, doctors to a large extent are taught to treat 'disease', not 'patients with disease'. I believe the doctor/patient *partnership* is vital in making all health care decisions.

Much of today's treatment is 'prophylactic' or preventive; not absolutely necessary but may improve the long-term outlook. Having surgery for appendicitis, which *must* be done to avoid catastrophe, is vastly different from taking medication to lower cholesterol, which *may* benefit the patient by reducing risk of heart attack over a period of many years. It is unwise to assume everything that *can* be done *should* be done in every circumstance since benefit and risk vary from patient to patient.

Many forms of disease today can be modified by a variety of treatments. Our history of fantastic medical successes has raised our life expectancy so we live longer. As we age, we develop disease and use the health care system more frequently. Much of what physicians and surgeons offer in terms of treatment is 'palliative'; we improve the symptoms, decrease the risk of complications and delay mortality. Today's chronic diseases challenge patients over many years; controlled but not cured.

Many of us remember a simpler time when we never questioned our doctor's authority. He alone possessed the knowledge. He made the decisions. We were not in a position to share in this responsibility. Times are changing. Attitudes are different. The pace is faster. The concepts of fast food and 30 minute pizza are now applied to all aspects of life. Everything is changing. Even traditional institutions are now different. Within the health care field, there is an evolution occurring which no one expected and few actually believe is happening. I am not referring to financial cutbacks and shorter hospital stays. I am referring to walk-in clinics and hospital emergency departments staffed by physicians who you may never meet again, family doctors who cannot handle more patients and hospital-based physicians (hospitalists) who are 'professional strangers' briefly responsible for your care during the sickest periods of your life.

Health care has become very fragmented. The system increasingly sponsors 'piece work' at the expense of 'continuity' in care; good care for the moment but inadequate attention to past or future medical concerns. Your health care record is fragmented and dispersed among a variety of health care 'outlets'; various doctor's offices, walk-in clinics, hospital emergency departments, etc. There exists no single health care record on you! Do not assume that these many health care outlets communicate with each other. If they try, it is not done well nor is it consistent. They are focused on the problem of the moment. Relatively cursory attention will be given to your health before or after the current problem. Although they are legally bound to keep a record of their interaction with you, they are not obligated to maintain your comprehensive medical record. Continuity of your medical care was once considered the highest priority. No longer! Your family physician managed your health care needs for a lifetime. No longer! Understand what I mean when I say fragmentation is rampant in the health care environment. The current system, given all of its successes, leaves the tracking of an individual's disease to that individual.

This book is designed to create Priority Patients who will not only survive, but who will master this environment and become less vulnerable. You can transform the doctor/patient relationships into a partnership. Consider presenting yourself to every physician as a willing and equal partner. Be prepared to share in the difficult decisions and understand that outcomes are not always predictable. Your approach will define the level of respect you have for each other. Even physicians unprepared to quickly accept this evolution will see the change in you and the potential for a more productive relationship.

Everything starts with your complaint, your symptom. Learn how to analyse your symptoms. Learn how to accurately and completely report these to a physician. The better you describe the complaint, the more focused will be the response. The more seriously your problem will be taken. You can dramatically improve the level of communication. This book will show you how critically important it is for you to clearly describe your symptom, understand your physician's response and jointly develop an approach. Your active participation will demonstrate your acceptance of personal responsibility. Your physician will soon recognise your efforts. This book will also teach you how to educate yourself about health care issues, make thoughtful health care decisions, monitor your performance and accurately record health care events.

Physicians help you with your medical problems. You are the only one who is responsible for your *long term* health care. No one can remember, record or monitor your entire health life. Perhaps the day will return when someone in the health care field will offer to do this for you. I doubt it! Certainly there will be new mechanisms developed for maintaining this record, but you will be the one responsible for its accuracy and completeness.

I want you to be a better health care consumer. I want you to be a better patient. I want you to take better care of yourself. I want you to ensure that your health care team takes better care of you. I want you to understand that health care is a personal responsibility; more today than ever before. I want you to learn to maintain your own medical health care diary. I will supply you with the tools to complete this task. You must ensure the integrity of your care, not just for the moment or the present problem, but ensure it for a life time of encounters with the medical establishment.

What I hope to accomplish with this book is to empower you to become a more educated, informed, and confident participant in the health care process. It is only by participating in, learning about, and taking an active role in your health life that you will maximize the benefits you receive from your interactions with health care professionals. If you become a knowledgeable and interested participant in the health care process, your health care team will be sure to treat you as a Priority Patient.

Dr. Ron Baigrie F.A.C.C., F.R.C.P.(C)

"Health care, no matter how technologically advanced it becomes, is a profoundly human experience. It is where we as individuals and family members must confront our own life, death and well-being, and that of the people we love. It is about me, the individual. But it is also about us, the collectivity"

Judith Maxwell
Canadian Medical Association Journal · June, 2002

Introduction To Your Symptom And You: The Best Kept Secret Of All Time

Once upon a time, many centuries ago, it was the general belief that the sun and the five known planets orbited around the earth. At the time, no one dared dispute Aristotle's or Ptolemy's concept that Earth was the central planet around which all others were in orbit. That is until Aristarchus of Samos proposed that the sun was the centre of the universe and that each new day was created by the single rotation of the earth on its axis. Aristarchus was ignored, and the incorrect theory of the geocentric (or Earth-centred) universe persisted for more than a thousand years. Copernicus successfully argued that Earth is not the centre of the universe; it simply revolves around the sun like all of the other known planets.

When one considers the current state of health care in North America, it is easy to draw parallels to early astronomy. The current system-focused method of delivering health care is geocentric in nature, and treats the patient as a minor planet in the health care universe. Patients (the sun) orbit around the system (the planets) as a matter of pure convenience for those who control the delivery of health care. While the various components of the current health care system are important, the patient is most important!

An ideal health care universe, would have a patient-focused method of delivering care; the patient (the sun) is at the centre, and the planets (doctors, nurses, hospitals, etc.) orbit around the patient. Health care providers *should* revolve around the patient servicing their needs and helping them return more quickly to a state of good health. Unfortunately this is currently not the case. So what happened? When did the patient become a secondary concern? What other large business puts its factories ahead of its customers?

Health Care Has Not Always Been Backwards!

Just as Aristarchus was once quite close to discovering the true nature of the universe, the health care systems of North American were once designed in a more patient-centred fashion. Health care used to consist of two components; the patient with their symptom and the doctor who brought them the treatment. The patient was the centre of the health care universe, and their symptom was the catalyst for all that followed. In effect, it could be argued that the symptom was the BIG BANG, from which the health care universe was created thus beginning the whole process. The doctor in those days would come to the patient and offer a treatment for their ailment that was tailored to suit their immediate needs as well as those in the future. The patient's lifestyle, background and personal issues were all taken into consideration when choosing a treatment strategy. The *whole* patient was the central consideration.

This concept of health care has sadly regressed to a system-centred universe wherein the system's concerns appear predominant. The various suns (or patients) revolve around the system (or Earth). Patients are seen as numbers, beds, procedures and diseases but rarely as individuals; until they identify themselves as such! Is the doctor waiting to see the patient or is the patient waiting.......?

The Modern Patient

Copernicus' great wisdom failed to reach the general public for many years, simply because he wrote in Latin; the language of the aristocracy. This book is written with *you* in mind, and it is designed to encourage the general public to adopt a form of 'Copernican' health care (health care with the patient at the centre) and live better and *safer* lives.

In the past, each person's focus was not on trying to live long and healthy lives; it was on pure survival, getting the next meal. Medical knowledge was special and even magical. Doctors and hospitals were even feared! Things are different now. The introduction of the Internet and the unhindered free access to medical knowledge alone has vastly changed how people perceive their health lives. There is no excuse in this day and age to not fully understand and have control of your health care. You have the best available knowledge, the maturity, intelligence and most of all, the vested interest! It is all about YOU! Isn't it a paradox that hospitals have multimillion-dollar budgets while at the same time, hundreds of thousands of patients are without a doctor? It simply makes no sense. Nurses and medical technologists get collective agreements. Doctors negotiate fee increases. Patients wait.

In order to bring patients, as well as the various health care components, into the twenty-first century, the universe as we know it must be redefined. We must ensure that output is more important than throughput. Our system has to recognize the *outcomes* of the patients being treated, not simply the *numbers* that can be quickly pushed through the system. LOS (length of stay) should be replaced by QOC (quality of outcome)! Each one of you is the key to changing the system for the better. Each one of you is the key to getting not only what you *want* from the health care system, but what you *need* from the health care system. Better patients will force a better system! A bigger system will not create better patients.

One of the main goals of this book is to teach you how to be a better, more efficient and more aware patient. It's aim is to empower you and teach you to question the order of your personal health care universe. It will show you how to become a Priority Patient. You will learn to expect care above and beyond what is commonly offered, and you will learn that nothing is perfect. You will also learn some 'street smarts' and negotiation tactics for managing your health life as well as learn how to maximize your benefits from contact with health care professionals. You will learn how to express yourself to the doctors and nurses as well as how to cooperate and participate in ways that will guarantee improved care!

Each section is comprised of smaller chapters titled *Secrets* or *Keys*. The secrets will give you some insights as to why the system works the way it does. It will give you the insider perspective of the current health care system. The keys will give you hints and tools to help you become a Priority Patient. There will be lists, points to follow, and questions to ask, to better prepare you for your encounters with the health care system. This book is designed to transform you from a passive observer into an active participant. It will depict typical patient issues and solutions, which help you navigate and succeed in the health care universe.

The Universe

Start to think of yourself as the centre of the universe....the health care universe. You must realize that you are the single most important component of the health care establishment. Without you and your illness, there would be no need for doctors, nurses, hospitals, health care statisticians or even the Minister of Health!

Each of you are (or at least should be) the primary focus of the health care business. Unfortunately, in a public health care system such as ours, this is not necessarily the case. In most businesses, customers or clients are valued because they make or break the business. In general the Canadian health care system does not treat its patients as valued customers. It treats them as excessive numbers of diabetics, heart attacks, coronary bypasses, and hysterectomies. Groups of individuals are lumped into statistics which are used to get funding for programs. Programs allow more focused and efficient care, facilitate research, and enable grouping of large numbers of patients while using the least amount of resources.

In this business, profit and success is measured by adhering to budgetary restrictions. This is frequently attained by limiting access to resources, for example the shortening of Length Of Stay (LOS), waiting lists, etc. In real (successful) business, profit is created by delivering the best products to the most clients consistently, with a smile!

If business measures success by the number of satisfied clients and high profits, then shouldn't the health care industry measure its success by the impact it has on people's lives? Is the pride of being on budget really a good measure of success? Most people would say no. Perhaps the health care industry could learn from big business and its practice of conducting market research to get input from its clients. Or, do they really care what you think? The Ontario Hospital report card may be a beginning.

Why is there not an outcry of rebellion against the imperfections, line-ups, waiting lists, delayed operations, and deaths? Are there not enough doctors, nurses, and equipment? WHY? Because people are both angry and frightened. Angry because they see deterioration in a system they have paid (prepaid) for. Fearful because of the "chill effect" that they may suffer from protesting the system's flaws. They are afraid that they will lose their doctor, their place in line, their priority on the waiting list, or that they will be treated differently. After all, this is Canada and (despite the fact that we are surrounded by water), Canadians don't like to make waves!!!

In The Beginning....

In the beginning there was no health care establishment; it simply was not needed. Then came you, you and you! The health care establishment developed as a response to your needs. You fell and cut yourself, woke up with belly pain, or your joints started to ache. You suffered a headache, a backache, neck pain or bleeding!

Doctors and nurses came to be because humans are vulnerable to illness and accidents. Like anything else, we developed a special group of people to handle illness and disease, just as we developed other specialists such as blacksmiths and bakers. Hospitals were created to respond to the problems of many sick and injured people. They quickly became places where people could be brought to the rapidly developing technology that in the twentieth century, was no longer portable.

Since people and their various problems were the instruments that started the entire process, why would the patient be considered anything but the centre of the health care universe? Just as it makes no sense to say that the sun should orbit around the planets, it equally makes no sense to say that the patient should orbit around the health care system. Why then does it happen every day? Why is so much time, money and effort spent finding a CEO for a hospital, while individual patients wait longer?

The Big Bang of the health care universe is you and your complaint. Without you and your medical problem, there is no need for the health care system! This is why you and your symptom are (or should be), the central focus of all activity in the health care universe.

Attention Class: 'The Patient Army' - A Unique Concept!

Patients represent the largest, most underestimated and underused component of the health care system. They are not the enemy! Contrary to what you might think, they are the 'troops' in this army fighting for health and the awareness of disease. Doctors, nurses and other health care professionals are the captains, majors, lieutenants and sergeants. Ministers of Health are the generals of the health care system.

While there are a very few generals and a decreasing number of officers, there are a growing number of patient troops. They are a renewable resource; an inexhaustible supply of 'recruits'. Just as good generals and officers know there can be no victory without well trained soldiers, so is it that the health care establishment will fail unless its patient/soldiers become well trained, knowledgeable, organized, self-sufficient and when necessary, able to understand and confront the enemy. The troops must have good leaders; leaders who understand that each 'soldier' has the potential to 'win a battle' by doing the right thing at the right time. They must both cooperate and use team spirit and initiative to win! Each patient should rise to the task of being a soldier not only to ensure their own protection and security, but also to share their knowledge and skills with others. Each of us has the most important role to play in our health care lives.

If the millions of troops do their part, not only will they be rewarded by better health, they will be rewarded by better health care. The diabetic patient should learn about her disease and how to treat it with diet, weight control, medications, self-testing, and administration of insulin. The patient with hypertension should learn to measure her blood pressure, avoid salt, take medications as prescribed, partake in regular exercise and learn not to smoke or be exposed to smoke. They should all learn to analyze and record symptoms, medical events, test results, medication dosages and changes. Many of them are not good soldiers.....yet!

Good patients do their very best to learn the why, how, when and what of their disease. They do what they can. Some are better that others. Some can lead. If they do not try, or if they ignore advice and teaching, they are bad soldiers. They will not perform well. Their safety and security are threatened. They will lose their battle! They might as well be AWOL (absent without leave)! Good soldiers become Priority Patients. They expect to be looked after but they share in looking after themselves. They have the best quality knowledge and tools available to them. The good ones will use the knowledge and tools to their benefit. They will 'share in their care'. The generals and officers will ensure that this knowledge is of high quality, readily available and easily understood by the soldiers. Generals and officers will create and supply the tools necessary for soldiers to be victorious in their individual battles. The knowledge and the tools and the high expectation of and pride in high-level performance, will lead to better outcomes and better relationships between the troops and their leaders.

We do not give medals of valour to our best patients. They are not rewarded by time off or special privileges. They receive their own reward, which is the best health and health care they can get. A good patient, a Priority Patient, is a patient who really cares about themselves and shows it, they have healthy life styles. Prevention is their passport. They enjoy the best possible relationships with their health care partners. They will be rewarded!

Many of you will be apprehensive in beginning this process. Everyone has a different personality and uses different techniques in communicating with others. How and when you start treating yourself as a Priority Patient and building a partnership with your physicians is for you to decide. We cannot predict when you will be ready, how you will interpret the contents of this book or how you will build your health care team. However, you will most assuredly use the same methods that have made you successful in all other aspects of your individual personal lives. Best of luck and convey our congratulations to all members of your health care team!

Secrets of The Big Bang

Let's imagine the ideal medical 'universe'. Our perspective is that the patient (the sun) is at the centre of this universe, with doctors, hospitals, walk-in clinics, nurses (the planets) orbiting about the patient. What started it all? The real universe is believed to have begun as an explosion/expansion of matter beginning from a single particle; the 'Big Bang'. By comparison, the individual patient's Big Bang is the onset of a complaint or a symptom. In fact it is the point of origin of the entire health care system; the moment after which all else begins. If there is no symptom, there is no contact with medical professionals, no diagnostic testing and no procedures. That is what makes your symptom so very important. That is what should make you the centre of the health care universe! The medical universe began as a *response* to people with symptoms and diseases. Unfortunately, the health care system has grown in size and has become so expensive that it appears to be the centre of its own universe.

Definitions

Symptoms: your complaints, the things that bother you and take you to your doctor for an explanation e.g. headache, fever, cough, etc.

Signs: an annoyance as much as a noticeable change in your body that may signal that something is wrong e.g. yellowing of the skin, rapid weight loss, water retention, etc.

Don't worry about what we call them; recognize them!

When people have symptoms they react. There may be little (if any), thought put into the analysis of the symptom until they are actually speaking with their physician face to face. Details are forgotten or become less than clear during the physician's interrogation. The process is much more complex and prolonged than need be. There are follow-up visits, repeat testing and many more inconveniences that in some cases can be avoided with a little forethought on the part of the patient.

Patients *must* recognize that describing symptoms to a physician is the most important part of seeking help for their complaint. When a physician is first confronted with a patient's symptoms, he must rely completely on the patient's description of the problem, obtained by asking questions. That is why what you do with your symptom plays a vital role in the health care process. It is the point of origin of the health care universe, a really big Bang!

Choices, Choices - You Make A Lot Of Them, But What About Your Health Care?

Making choices regarding your health may seem difficult, but you do it every day. You decide to smoke or not, to take drugs or not, to gain weight or not, see a doctor or not, take the doctor's advice or not, etc., etc. You decide how you will react to a new symptom. Once you mention it to family or friends, you expect advice or council.

For example, one day you wake up and start your car and you hear a noise. There are a series of actions that you may take. Some people will ignore it, others lift the hood and attempt to locate and investigate it. If this does not help, they may take it to a mechanic. At the garage, they describe the noise to the mechanic. The mechanic may want to run some diagnostic tests. It is obvious that the possible outcomes are limitless. It all starts with the driver. The driver must take responsibility for his vehicle. The responsibility of making the situation (as well as his wishes) clear to the mechanic lies with the driver!

It's Not Black Or White - Sometimes It's Not Even Grey!

Unfortunately it is not always easy to interpret and describe symptoms. In fact, to complicate matters further, symptoms may or may not mean disease and diseases may or may not produce symptoms. It can be compared to driving a car with loose steering, a worn bearing, a loose tie rod and an almost flat tire; all of these will affect your steering, but how do you know which one it is or indeed if there is only one problem? Likewise, having a radiator leak at the same time as a malfunctioning thermostat allows unrecognized overheating until it is too late.

The best problem-solving device for the diagnostic process is a lengthy and accurate description of symptoms; how they started, in what order, how often they occur and similar distinguishing information that only the patient can provide. For example, if a patient walks in and simply says, "It hurts and I don't feel well", the doctor has very little to go on. On the other hand, if the patient walks in and says, "I started having a crushing chest pain last night about five minutes after I began running", the doctor has much more specific problem-focused information to process. He is far more likely to proceed in the right direction in pursuit of an accurate diagnosis.

Taking The Patient History - Describing Your Personal Big Bang!

Some physicians are naturally better at questioning patients. They get their information from their patients thoroughly and with relative ease. They take their time and get the story in the patient's own words. Others may make it seem like an interrogation! If the doctor ignores the patient's details, he may miss a key component and be led in the wrong direction.

Being a good historian is not an easy task. People are quite different from one another, and getting them to speak about their complaint can require a variety of techniques. Some patients talk too much (without offering relevant details), and others speak far too little. A good physician can get what they need from a patient in a reasonable amount of time without being consumed by the details about Great-Great-Aunt Bertha.

Patients can derail the examination process by 'chatting', or even attempting to direct the doctor toward a preferred diagnosis. They neglect to give the doctor important details of their *actual* problem, but give him personal theories about *their* diagnosis instead. Always keep to the description of symptoms and stick to the facts!

The Patient - Noticing The Signs

Many symptoms are ignored or forgotten. You should not only be noticing your symptoms and recording them, but you should also get to know your body. Anything you perceive to be abnormal or any change you cannot explain is referred to as a "sign". You should be able to recognize tell-tail signs that appear indicating that there is something wrong. Some such signs are:

Signs Of Illness

- Loss of appetite
- Swelling
- Frequent urination
- Diarrhea or constipation
- Blood in stools
- Changes in skin colour
- Irregular heart beats
- Abnormal weight loss
- Decrease in energy
- Change in appearance of mole
- Appearance of a lump

Your best defence against 'silent killers' is awareness. You are the only one who knows your body. Ignored or forgotten symptoms and signs can affect your care later. An single episode of flu causing temporary diarrhea is vastly different than six months of unexplained diarrhea.

Doctors - Reading The Signs!

The interpretation of signs by physicians is quite different. Doctors use signs to help diagnose the presence or absence, type and extent of disease. This explains why your doctor must conduct a physical examination as well as a detailed patient history. Along with a description of their symptoms, *tangible* signs of a patient's illness can be very helpful to the diagnostic process. You may wonder why your doctor pokes and prods you during your visit. They are looking for *physical* clues to your problem. The eyes, hands, chest, and mouth can give a doctor a great deal of information about a patient's condition and the extent of disease.

When your physician is looking for abnormalities or physical signs of illness, they are searching for the cause of your symptom. For example, blood pressure is a marker of a problem with your circulatory system, just as a rattle in your chest may mean a respiratory problem. Physical signs help your doctor to further narrow down the possibilities.

In The Beginning - There Was The Symptom....

It all starts with the symptom. The symptom is the Big Bang. It is the beginning or the flash point of the entire health care process. It is your very personal and individual 'entry' into the health care universe. It is often the ambiguity or lack of understanding of the symptom that leads to misdiagnosis, incorrect treatment, wrong medication, unnecessary diagnostic testing and wasteful, potentially dangerous practices.

Doctors need to understand the symptom clearly, as it is their most important tool to discovering the cause behind the complaint. Frequently it is difficult to identify the specific cause of a symptom. This can result in a trial-and-error treatment process often confusing and difficult for the patient to comprehend. Patients should not always expect a precise diagnosis.

If not treated with the seriousness it deserves, the symptom can lead you and your doctor down the wrong path. You and your doctor must develop a clear road map from the start, or your problem-solving journey will be difficult and confusing. So be careful – think about your symptom before you act!

Keys To Your Symptoms

Symptoms are the same to your doctor as clues are to a detective. They play a vital role in the process of diagnosis and treatment. It is astounding how little significance patients place on their symptoms. This is the biggest mistake a patient can make. Both doctor and patient should spend a significant amount of time exploring and defining the symptom. Why? Because the description of the patient's symptom represents the most important clue to discovering if anything is wrong. It is very important to appreciate that symptoms do not always indicate the presence of disease. Any symptom can indicate either a serious disease process or merely a mild functional abnormality. The art of this process is to get the best clues from the description of the symptom and use these to solve the mystery.

Personal Responses To Symptoms

Many thousands of people develop ailments of one type or another every day. These complaints can range from simple headache, heartburn, palpitation, cough, etc., all the way to massive heart attack or serious bleeding. How each individual reacts to these symptoms will dictate the treatment they receive. Some patients rush immediately to the emergency room only to be told it is not important. Others will ignore their complaint until several months have passed before they are diagnosed with a serious disease. Each of us individually decides how we react to our symptoms. It is a form of self-diagnosis and self-treatment without any formal training! This self-care process cannot be replaced, but it can be improved.

There are an unlimited number of possibilities that can be chosen depending on the symptom, the individual patient, the current circumstances and history of the patient. The processes for deciding what actions will be taken can be illustrated with a decision tree. Not all people react to similar symptoms in a similar manner. We may do all, some or none of the following:

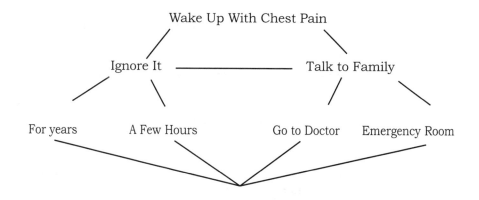

A decision is not necessarily the right one or the wrong one, simply very personal. We may not even be consistent; today we ignore them, the next time we take them to the doctor. Sometimes, we handle symptoms at home. At other times, we *medicalize* our symptoms, by that we mean taking them to a doctor.

In this book we will not tell you how or when to act on your symptom.
That would be irresponsible.

Should you choose to medicalize your symptom, and you wish to have a productive visit to your doctor's office, then what should you do? You participate in the process. Remember it's your symptom, your problem, your responsibility to clearly communicate it to your doctor. The better the clues, the more likely the 'crime' will be solved. In every other aspect of life we prepare ourselves: buying a car, selecting clothing, remodelling the house. We weigh our options, we list our needs, and then clearly present them to the sales people. We rarely put this amount of thought into describing our symptoms; this has to change! Many patients show up at the doctor's office and cannot even remember the details of their complaint! You now know the necessity of good clues.

Just as with other decisions in your life, you should make a mental record of your complaint and then sit down with pen and paper and record this vital information for your physician. You might consider getting started by completing a 'symptom form' describing the characteristics of your complaint. Your list may include:

Recording Your Symptoms

- When the problem occurred and how often
- How long it lasted
- How severe it was
- Which other symptoms occurred at the same time
- What brought on the complaint
- What relieved it
- One good descriptive word to explain the problem
- Activities that preceded the problem
- The first time it occurred
- Results of any previous treatments
- If it is disabling

The details you supply are vital in providing the physician a firm starting place to guide him in his pursuit of an answer.

Our point in this exercise is to improve communication with your physician once you have decided to seek his advice.

Before you go to your doctor, you should be prepared. Think about and record the description of your symptom, and write down any questions you may have.

Reacting To It - What You Do And Why (Sometimes You're Not Even Sure)!

We make choices about our health and health care all the time. Some of these lead us to seek medical advice. Some of us are over-reactors and some of us are under-reactors. We all have a different threshold for acting and reacting.

Symptoms That Are Not To Be Ignored!

- persistent fever
- blood in bowel movement
- recurrent diarrhea
- coughing up yellow-green phlegm
- coughing up blood
- vomiting up blood
- chest pain
- recurrent headache
- persistent infection

No one can tell you precisely if or when you should seek medical advice. It's all a matter of educating yourself, thinking things through and making a *choice*. You can do much to minimize your contact with physicians by healthy living. Even if you think your complaint is trivial, it may still be in your best interest to confirm that with your physician, thus avoiding persisting concern and being prepared for the next time.

Since every individual's personality, level of confidence, need for reassurance, education, intelligence, etc., plays a large part in their decision to seek medical advice, it is difficult to say how they will react in any given circumstance. The 65-year-old executive (who has suffered 2 previous heart attacks) ignores his chest pain all day long only to be rushed to the emergency room that evening in the throws of a major heart attack;

he did not make a good decision. It is the individual who must weigh their personal information against other factors and make the choice. It is your health; choose wisely! When you have chosen to share your symptoms with the medical world, remember: the symptom is most critical to the process.

Now You know Why Your Doctor Asks So Many Questions!

Your visit to the doctor's office will only be a success if you do your part and participate in the healing process. This means that you need to do the following:

- Record.
- Describe.
- Understand.
- Make decisions about your symptoms.
- Realize that two symptoms may be unrelated and indicate two or more separate problems.

If you do this in detail and as accurately as possible, your doctor has a better chance of recognizing the problem. If not, then the doctor's job becomes much more difficult and he must question you endlessly to get this information. That's why it is referred to as "taking a history" rather than "receiving a history"! Some patients tell better stories than others.

A doctor's first obligation should be to attempt to understand not only what the patient is suffering from, but understand the rest of the patient as well. They must process all of the information that they receive about the patient (especially the description of their symptoms) and attempt to 'rule in' or 'rule out' a diagnosis. You can appreciate how it is much like solving a crime. If the clues are clear and concise, then it is easy to solve. If they are too few or confusing, then the mystery becomes more difficult to solve.

What Your Doctor Does And Why?

Many different diseases present with very similar complaints and many complaints can have multiple sources. For example, simple chest pain can be caused by a problem with your heart, lungs, digestion, stomach, muscles, bones, etc. This can lead to a number of interpretations by your physician. He must ask you to clearly state the problem. This examination process should involve a sufficient number of questions to identify the potential source of your complaint. This must be a thorough process. It should take as long as necessary. Too short a time can be dangerous.

Doctors may proceed in a variety of fashions, all of which depend on how well they know you personally and how well they interpret your description of your complaint. Some ways that your doctor may proceed might be:

Your Doctor's Options

- Continue to ask you more questions.
- Get confirmation from your spouse or friend.
- Do a diagnostic test (to get objective information).
- Question your motives.
- Order a second test.
- Have you return another day to reassess.
- Offer a trial therapy (try a medication).
- Admit that they don't have an answer.
- Discover the problem and treat it.

Once again, the entire process begins with a good description of your complaint! The more clear and concise you are, the better chance the doctor has of getting it right. It used to be said that the diagnosis could be made 70% of the time based on a good patient history and description of the symptom. Diagnosis and treatment can sometimes be accomplished as quickly as you can accurately describe your symptoms!

Your Personal Physician Plays A Vital Role!

Don't believe for one minute that any doctor will do. Nothing can replace a continuous physician/patient partnership. If you are fortunate, your personal physician knows you well and already has many of the clues in place. If you are seeing a physician who does not know you (more common today), he needs to assess not only the symptom but you the person. The process of getting on the correct path can be quite complicated. Unfortunately, the physician has as many if not more decisions to make than the patient does at the onset of their problem. There are unlimited diagnostic and treatment options to pursue; all of which should have input from the patient. Your symptoms dictate what happens next!

✱ ✱ ✱ ✱ ✱

"The patient now is seen as an important part, a 'partner' is his or her own health care"

Dr. Adeline Falk-Rafael

Toronto Star • November, 2002

Chapter Summary

- Your symptom is the key!

- You are the first in charge!

- How you *act* tells them how to *react!*

- Get involved in your complaint!

- Know the little details!

- Be involved in the choices!

- Record, record, record!

- Become an active participant!

- Some symptoms are more serious than others!

- Taking your history can seem like an interrogation - the more clues the better!

Keys To Calling For Help

People often feel intimidated about calling for help. Even in the throws of a heart attack, some will drive themselves to the hospital or have a family member drive them. This may not be the best choice. While it may save time, the life saving abilities of an untrained, occupied driver are nonexistent. Compare that to the capabilities of specialized paramedic personnel who are trained and equipped to administer emergency medical care in the ambulance on route to the hospital. Choose wisely!

Never be afraid to call for help!

It is difficult for ordinary people to decide when and how to call for help. These choices and decisions are random and personal. You may not realize just how critical your situation really is. While most of us don't want to abuse expensive facilities, we shouldn't take unnecessary chances with our lives simply to avoid embarrassment and cost. Deciding how to respond and what action to take when you or a loved one is sick, can be among the most stressful of choices. You feel pressure to make decisions and take action. Analysing your symptoms is essential in deciding how to react. Do not underestimate the tremendous importance attached to your description of your symptom. You are not trained to do this. It's never easy.

Who Can You Call?

There are many services that you can contact when you need help. There are services such as Telehealth Ontario that help patients by encouraging them to clearly describe their symptoms and then offer advice regarding appropriate action based on those descriptions. Each of these services is designed to respond to your call for assistance. They ask you for specific details regarding your complaint in order to decide how 'serious' the problem could be. Widely accepted protocols are used to handle specific complaints. For example if your chest pain sounds like you are having a heart attack, they will likely dispatch an ambulance to your home. On the other hand, if your rash has been present for three weeks they will probably advise you to see your doctor within a few days. You should now realize the importance of the detailed information you convey to the information 'hotline'. The details you supply will significantly affect the advice you are given. You will not find this process as simple as calling the fire department when you have a fire!

Your Doctor or Specialist - If You Have One!

It is a good idea to clarify with your doctor or specialist what type of practice they have, what their availability is during and after hours and how they would like you to act when you feel you need urgent or immediate help. All too often, when you need advice, it is after regular office hours. In those circumstances, you will get your doctor's telephone answering service advising you to go to the emergency department if you need immediate help. Even during regular office hours, you may well be told to go to the emergency department. In some cases, if you call your doctor's office they will provide you with information on what to do if it is a problem with which they are familiar. If you have been under their care for a long-standing condition, they may offer you specific advice (e.g. regarding medications). In the case of your specialist, they usually do not offer services after hours, but may help you if he is familiar with your problem. If you are participating in a research trial you should have a number to call 24 hours a day, seven days a week.

Specific Hotlines

There are many emergency specific hotlines available to call. All phone books should have emergency hotline numbers for the local area. If they do not, you can call information (411) and request the number of the service for which you are looking, or call 1-800-555-1212 and request a 1-800 number for the service you require. We recommend that you list your local emergency hotline numbers in an easily accessible location.

Emergency Hotlines

- Poison Control
- Assault Victims (Assaulted women's help line, Child Abuse help line)
- Drug and Alcohol treatment info-line
- Kids Help Phone
- Parent Help Line
- Teen Hotline
- Telehealth Ontario (or similar provincial health lines)
- Registered Nurse Hotline
- Your local Emergency department

Many of these services are designed to help you assess your problem and its severity, and help you decide on what course of action you should take.

Please note that if you call the local hospital emergency department they will respond to your request according to hospital policy; detailed advice from nursing staff may not be allowed. There are exceptions. Pregnant patients for example, may receive special instructions or be transferred to a nurse in the maternity ward. In all cases, you are likely to be referred to a specific hotline. If the hospital policy permits, they may respond by telling you to come in. Don't expect to talk to a doctor.

Operators And 911

If you recognize that the condition is severe and potentially life threatening (e.g. heart attack, severe bleeding) the best option is to call your local operator (by dialling "0"), or if your region is equipped, call 911 immediately. The 911 operator will notify the appropriate emergency service. They will usually keep you on the line in order to monitor the situation until help arrives. Unfortunately they do not have the ability to offer medical advice except in the most limited sense (i.e. general first aid recommendations). If necessary they will notify the police or fire department. It is not uncommon for the fire department to respond in small communities since they are trained in first aid and Cardio Pulmonary Resuscitation (CPR).

What Will They Say?

In most cases, the following is true; they will always supply you with the safest advice even if it is excessive. This is not a bad thing; it simply means that you should not necessarily be frightened by an operator or nurse's decision to send help or request that you get to the emergency room quickly. They must be careful because it is impossible to accurately diagnose a condition over the phone. Hotline personnel must suggest that you seek medical advice even if you remotely resemble the typical profile (as determined by algorithms and questionnaires) of a person in need of medical attention. Remember, you will eventually have to decide how to act in each situation. Use the hotlines for advice.

Preparing For Emergency Medical Personnel (Ambulance, etc.)

If your call for help has resulted in an ambulance bring dispatched, there are several steps you can take to prepare. When the emergency personnel arrive they will question you to obtain the necessary information. This will not be the slow and careful interview that you have experienced in your doctor's office. This will be fast-paced questioning that requires either yourself or a family member/friend be ready with the answers.

Before they arrive you would be well advised to record some of the following information:

Write It Down

- Your symptoms in detail
- History of the problem (has it happened before? –when, where, etc.)
- Names of your doctors and specialists
- Phone number of someone you want contacted
- Description of the pain on a scale of 1 to 10 (1 being no pain and 10 being the worst pain you can possibly imagine)
- Record other major medical problems that you currently have (e.g. pacemaker, etc.) and list your allergies (especially those to medication).
- Record the time and type of your last food and fluid.

There are a number of things you should do to prepare for their arrival:

Have It Ready

- Get your medication bottles together and show them to the paramedics or emergency personnel. You will need to show them to the emergency room nurses and doctors as well.
- Follow any instructions given by the operator.
- Bring your personal health care diary (along with advance directives).
- Bring your health card and copies of your identification (remember never to bring original I.D. with the exception of your health card).

Take It With You

- Pack a change of clothes for your return from the hospital (you never know what can happen to the clothes you are wearing!).
- Remove your valuables and leave them at home.
- Remove your dentures and/or glasses and pack them in a safe place.
- Bring some money (in the form of change) but not more than $20.00.

Being prepared will make it much easier for others to help you. You can't be sure that you will be able to communicate with others (especially if you become unconscious), so write things down and keep your personal health care diary up to date! Nobody in the E.R. minds if you go home treated for a minor problem that you *thought* might be a major one. They are as happy and relieved as you are. This is particularly true for children.

Chapter Summary

- If you are not sure, it's your CALL!

- Don't feel you are wasting their time.

- No one thinks it will happen to them, so be prepared!

- Don't panic!

- Be ready for questions.

- Describe your complaint clearly in detail.

- Don't exaggerate, but don't leave things out!

- It is better to get the help you need than to think you can do it alone!

Before...

... AFTER

Introduction To Doctors And You: The Changing Doctor/Patient Relationship

We have witnessed rather remarkable changes in the doctor patient relationship during the last twenty years. The "frontier" doctor who made house calls, handled both minor ailments and serious emergencies as well as caring for entire families from birth to death is now a rare individual. For a variety of reasons he evolved from the traditional 'family physician'. Gone are the days when such a family physician alone, knows all there is to know about every medical condition. It is more complicated today. For a while he acted as the quarterback for an expanded team of health care professionals, each playing their part in the care of an individual patient. Unfortunately this practice is dissolving. The role of the family physician as quarterback is frequently ignored by doctors and patients alike. Care becomes fragmented when patients seek advice from doctors on call, walk-in clinics, emergency rooms, nurse practitioners, etc. However, such behaviour is often unavoidable since the family doctor's office is only open from 9 to 5. Do you see a problem developing here?

This change in the doctor/patient relationship is not all that surprising. If your personal physician is not available, you seek help elsewhere. The modern day health care 'team' is frequently disconnected by this evolutionary process. Who's on the team? Are the team members communicating with one another? Do they know you that well? Is your personal physician acting as the captain of this team? If not, who is? You? Some patients are either not interested in or are unable to maintain an ongoing professional relationship with a personal physician. Sadly, 'Rent-a-doc' is just around the corner – if not already here! This 'drive-through' approach to your health care may be convenient but also dangerous. For the time being, it appears to represent a necessary evil.

You Have Great Players, But Where's The Coach?

As with any professional team, you may have the best players available. However, if the members of your team are not working together, you could lose the game. This analogy applies nicely to health care today. You could have the best family physician, the best specialist and the best surgeon, but if each of them is approaching your problem from a different perspective, it only looks like you're getting great care, when maybe you're not!

Medical knowledge has exploded! The complexity of health care today requires the input from an expanded team of professionals, each with a specific area of expertise. Their coordinated participation in your care is more important than you can possibly imagine!

Doctors must work in teams to ensure that they have all the bases covered. Patients should actively participate, not just expect that their problems are taken care of as quickly as possible. Participation means much more. Life is fast-paced and we seem to want fast-paced care. Be careful! The loss of the once important 'continuity of care' guaranteed by a well-established doctor/patient relationship leaves the patient vulnerable. In the absence of such a relationship, patients risk becoming faceless, nameless, generic humanoids subjected to a piecework approach. Concentrating on the problem or the disease of the moment and isolating this from the patient ignores other extremely important components of the individual, a process that can lead to errors and misconceptions.

If you want to be perceived as a Priority Patient, you must ensure that you are treated as a complete individual and not just a disease entity. This new attitude will set you apart and guarantee that you are accepted as an active participant. Believe it or not, doctors will eventually respond positively to patients who take an active interest in their health care. Why be treated like a number when you should be treated like a human being.

Who Is The Captain?

Every team must have a captain, someone who keeps the communication lines open, keeps all of the players informed and coordinates the plays. You could fill this role. Why not? It is after all your life! If successful, you are now more than just a participant; you are in charge. Remember, the members of your health care team have different backgrounds and training. Each of them comes at you from their point of view. You must ensure that they all have a similar focus, the same goal in mind and take the appropriate actions to give you the care you need and to achieve the results you are hoping for. If you decide to actively participate (or even co-ordinate), you reduce the depersonalization that occurs when several professionals become involved in your care. Treatment should always be tailored to suit the patient.

The New Doctor/Doctor/Doctor/Patient Relationship

There is a new system of health care. There are specialists, sub-specialists and even sub-sub-specialists, most of whom will be strangers. Take heart disease for example. A common scenario might consist of: patient sees family doctor, then diagnostic cardiologist, then cardiologist who does angiograms, next a cardiologist who does angioplasty, then a cardiologist who does rehabilitation. Confusing eh? While this new system has many benefits (such as access to various opinions, information and health care professionals), it fragments the care. The patient gets good care, but it comes in pieces which must be fit together (like a puzzle). Who better qualified to put and keep it together than you?

A truly beneficial doctor/patient relationship must begin with excellent communication. All doctors have attained a certain level of training in order to be in their current position. They have all achieved a certain understanding of basic medical principals. However, this knowledge applied incorrectly due to miscommunication can lead to an unexpected outcome. Communication is the key to excellent health care. Priority Patients should always attempt to do the following:

Good Medicine

- Form a meaningful relationship with their physician
- Ensure the doctor explains the diagnosis and treatment options.
- Encourage participation of loved-ones in the decision-making process.
- Discuss their medical issues, personal concerns and even fears with the physician
- Expect to understand, in detail, treatment options.
- Ask questions and clarify concerns before proceeding with treatment strategies.
- Match the treatment to the problem proportionally (they should not fix a flat tire by overhauling the engine!).

Patients need to feel that they are treated with respect, have a thorough discussion and examination, understand the diagnosis, know the treatment options and management plan. This is the bottom line. It may not mean that the patient improves, or is cured, but an important part of good health care is that the patient feels satisfied.

Satisfaction does not imply you have received the best of care or the most of care; it means that you have understood and agreed to the treatment you have received and the direction in which you and your doctor are going. Failure of any of these elements can lead to both bad medicine and/or dissatisfaction. What good is an expensive diagnostic test if it has no bearing on the outcome of the patient's health? What good is an excellent physician by reputation if you are treated without kindness and respect? What good is knowing the treatment options if you are forced to take the one the doctor wants?

A good doctor/patient relationship will be initiated and driven by the patient. Remember, you have one doctor, he has hundreds of patients! In a good doctor/patient relationship there are few misunderstandings. If things don't turn out as expected, it's likely not a question of fault. If both parties truly understand the risks and benefits of the chosen treatment strategy (which they should), neither should feel that they have been mislead. A clear understanding is the product of an ideal doctor/patient relationship.

Review the highlights of this introduction.

1) **Each of us will decide our level of participation based on who we are.**

2) **Plan to be the captain, the coach or a player on the bench.**

3) **Take charge of your team or hand over control to a stranger again, again and again.**

4) **Decide on the level of participation with which you are comfortable.**

5) **Form a lasting doctor/patient relationship.**

6) **Take responsibility for your share of the decisions.**

7) **Doctors do their best – patients should too.**

8) **Treatment outcomes are *expected* not *guaranteed*!**

* * * * *

"Open and honest communication is a prerequisite for good relationships which in turn, build trust. Trust is what family practice is all about. So communicating better [is] step one"

Dr. Patricia Mark
Medical Post · November, 2001

Secret Factors That Influence Your Doctor

The current system is undergoing tremendous growing pains. Almost every facet of the medical universe is changing in one manner or other. It is increasingly obvious that our health care system is under great stress. Those who *use* the system know it; those who haven't used the system lately may not realize it. Our high quality health care cannot be sustained under this ever-growing burden. We are desperately in need of change. However, it must be a change that will *maintain* the quality and *relieve* the burden.

It is both fortunate and unfortunate that change is an evolutionary process. Some of the 'quick fixes' of the past have led to many of today's problems. Lack of sufficient health care personnel created by cutting training positions for nurses and doctors years ago, is but one example. Perhaps the greatest burden is that there are more people alive today with *chronic* diseases; we are indeed the victims of our own successes. Keeping people alive with disease is both expensive and time consuming. Treating an older patient for 15 years after a coronary bypass operation is vastly different than treating a younger patient for pneumonia, which is cured in 10 days. Similarly, new drugs and high-tech equipment will continue to consume much of our health care budget because they represent the product of our fantastic medical achievements.

What is required now is a long-term plan that ensures high-quality health care for all patients. There have been and continue to be many proposed solutions: more money, privatization, user fees, de-listing of insured services, salaried physicians, nurse practitioners, fewer beds, and finally....even more money. The only way that things can change for the better is if we examine what is happening with the present system and attempt to understand what is wrong with it. Such examinations have not been rare. This one has a different perspective.

Your doctor and therefore your care is continually influenced by a variety of changing trends and new discoveries. The trends we are going to show you are examples of how the system deals with *groups* of patients and diseases and not with *individuals*. Think about these trends (or what I call experiments) as honest efforts to improve our health care system but with the unfortunate ultimate impact of depersonalizing the individual. In the past as a society we learned to believe that medicine was an infallible science not subject to human whims or trends. You may feel different at the end of this chapter. As you read on consider whether you are being treated as an individual or as a member of a group.

New Discoveries

Our health care establishment is constantly pursuing newer and better approaches to diagnosis and treatment. Indeed physicians who are not familiar with and utilize these new techniques are deemed outdated. We have been trained to believe that only the newest is the best. The MRI scan is better than the CT scan, the new x-ray dye is better than that old dye. It's a bit like saying that a 1998 car is better than a 1996 model and it might be in some ways, but it costs $2000.00 more and it's still a car. It may have a new appearance but it will still rust, only get you where you are going and the speed limit does not change. In other words, we sometimes pay a great deal more money for minimal improvement. Perhaps we want the new car for other reasons, not just for driving.

Historically, medicine has made both incredible leaps forward and experienced terrible set backs as a result of medical trends. Scientists have made tremendous advancements in medicine because they are pioneers, explorers and craftsmen. It is difficult to imagine, but the first *blood transfusion* done by Jean Denys (of France) on the 25 of June 1667, was actually done using calf's blood strictly because of the animal's 'gentle nature'. It was thought that animal's blood would be more pure than human blood, because animals were not prone to the same vice of drinking as were humans. Over 200 years later, after many studies showed evidence to the contrary, doctors such as Franz Gesellius and Oscar Hasse were still performing animal to human transfusions! Today of course, we realize how silly this logic seems.

Astounding medical achievements have not come without cost. Not infrequently a mistakenly great idea has become a sweeping trend (temporarily) only to be eventually recognized as incorrect. One example is the Vineberg operation; a surgical procedure that plunged the internal thoracic artery directly into heart muscle hoping an actual coronary bypass would result. But trends are powerful things. We would not have nearly the number of incredible advances in medicine if it were not for scientists and patients willing to pursue new ideas and practices, some of which will revolutionize medicine and some of which will appropriately disappear.

Unfortunately trends created by great ideas have sometimes had negative effects. The trends toward treatments once deemed absolutely necessary (radical mastectomy vs. lumpectomy, hormone replacement therapy, breast self-examination, tonsillectomies, varying rates of hysterectomy and cesarean births) are examples of the cost of learning. The value of these historically trendy approaches is now actively debated. It is easy to see how trendy the 'science' of medicine can be!

In the beginning, a trend represents the acceptance of a fantastic new idea, which is enthusiastically adopted in practice. In time, these new ideas are so good they either force global change or are recognized as failures and vanish. The overuse of trendy diagnostic and treatment strategies is very common as part of the early enthusiasm phase and is unnecessarily expensive. In this regard, doctors and scientists are acting out the human role of consumer. Buyer beware!

Evidence Based Medicine

One of the latest results of scientific study is the clinical experiment known Evidence Based Medicine (EBM). The Evidence Based Medicine movement dictates that doctors should deliver health care (diagnostic and therapeutic) based on knowledge obtained by scientific study. The concept is that the physician is aware of the available scientific data and applies that knowledge in his routine decision-making process. Please note, most scientific data comes from studies on *groups* of patients. Decision-making by a physician always involves an *individual* patient. Ideally the physician is capable of applying group-based data to individual patients. The concept implies improved care for all patients but *not necessarily* so.

Unfortunately, as you will come to understand, the interpretation of scientific data and its clinical application to individual patients is a continuing challenge. The requirements for this process are: a physician who understands the science, honest and transparent presentation of the data, understandable scientific publications, minimal media hype, full disclosure of *all* the data, clear implications for the individual as well as the group. Obviously the most important component is an interested patient who understands why the doctor is choosing a particular test or treatment.

There is a tendency to not have all of the above components, in the day-to-day decision-making process. For example, data can be presented and published in a biased fashion making the results appear favourable for all individuals when they are only shown to be favourable for large groups of patients. Some doctors have difficulty with data and its interpretation. There are many ways of presenting data so that it looks far more impressive than it is. If published data from clinical trials were to be followed blindly, without allowing for individualization, many patients would receive unnecessary tests and treatment. Interpretation of test results and clinical trials requires a 'dose' of both tremendous skill and skepticism.

Scientific studies released with excessive media hype will automatically encourage enthusiastic acceptance by doctors and patients – right or wrong! Incomplete release of all the data from a trial may favour the use of new treatments in the wrong situations (not everyone with high cholesterol needs a cholesterol-lowering drug!). Trials that show that large groups of patients who respond to treatment generally fail to point out that many individuals in those groups did not benefit from that treatment. The resulting 'carpet bombing' effect requires that *many* patients must receive treatment in order to find the *one* who will definitely benefit. By the way, we never know who that one is! Who really is being treated; the group or the individual? The term 'number needed to treat', defines the necessity to treat many patients in order to benefit a few.

Treatment Algorithms And Clinical Pathways

A recently emerging experiment is know as the *treatment algorithm*. As an example, if you go to an emergency department with a complaint such as chest pain, the staff will immediately begin a management process, based primarily on the complaint, not you. This process will consist of a specific history, examination, blood tests, ECG, and probably a chest x-ray. Depending on the results of these tests, another series of actions will be taken. If you have had a heart attack the actions taken will be different than if you have indigestion. Note that the actions taken are in response to the complaint, not the individual with the complaint. Each hospital may have its own version of these pre-defined diagnostic and treatment pathways. It can be argued that they are primarily designed to: effectively deal with your complaint, move you through the emergency department more quickly, more efficiently deal with your hospitalization.

Born in the name of efficiency, the *treatment algorithm* and its close cousin, the *clinical pathway* can effectively remove individual interpretation and decision–making from the diagnostic process. In other words, when you go to the emergency room, the health care worker who is treating you will follow a specific set of guidelines based on your answers to a few simple questions rather than just relying on their clinical experience and personal instincts. This is intended to ensure that all patients with a certain complaint receive a standard level of care. This approach can be problematic for those whose complaints are vague and non-specific. Why this approach? It identifies costs, it defines a standard of care, it simplifies approach, improves efficiency, allows for audit, alleviates pressure in chaotic environments and ultimately protects the institutions and to some extent patients from medical-legal involvement. Sounds bureaucratic doesn't it!

Is there a down side? There could be. Terrible things can happen to chest pain patients who enter the emergency room and *do not* have heart disease. They may be admitted to hospital and undergo a battery of tests (some of which expose them to risks). If the source of their pain is not identified, despite all of these tests, there may be frequent recurrences. Many patients with chest pain become quite confused following this experience and may be simply released to go home without a diagnosis but told to return if it recurs. This approach is not logical, nor does it address the real problem.

Obeying the algorithm does not necessarily help the patient. Do algorithms always help? NO! However, the patient who is having a subtle heart attack may be rewarded by having the algorithm correctly diagnose their condition. Is it the patient or the algorithm that's being treated?

For many years, physicians were respected for their wisdom. They alone had the clinical experience and the knowledge to help their patients. The application of algorithms and clinical pathways (particularly in hospital) has the potential to remove clinical experience and accumulated wisdom from the equation. After all, the analysis of test results and data created by the algorithm, does not factor in features of the individual patient; the single algorithm is applied to *all* patients. The art of medicine has always been the ability to interpret test results and data with full knowledge of the individual patient. Today, doctors spend less time questioning and examining patients. They scrutinize test results with vigour. It is now common that 30% of coronary angiograms are normal indicating a need to investigate and apply high-tech, risky diagnostic techniques to patients who do not have heart disease. Collateral damage? What will be the impact on future generations of health care personnel if they are taught to apply algorithms and clinical pathways to groups of patients with complaints? This is vastly different than the traditional doctor/patient relationship.

Changing Practice Patterns And Attitudes

Doctors used to be in charge of the medical universe. Unfortunately, nurses were subservient. Doctors until recently have generally been self-employed entrepreneurs whose primary concern was patient care. Nurses have always been in the role of employee. As hospitals became larger, more numerous and more complex, and increasingly more expensive, the management of the system shifted into the hands of trained administrators away from physicians lacking the necessary skills. Hospitals are now large corporations (bureaucracies) with thousands of employees. Some nurses as salaried employees of hospitals moved into increasingly senior management positions. Doctors on the other hand, apply for and receive 'annual privileges' to practice within the hospital. In Canada there is a movement to limit the monetary income of physicians since they represent a large expense for the system. Placing physicians on alternative payment plans (salary) as opposed to the tradition of fee-for-service has become a system objective.

These changes have had profound effects on attitudes within the health care system. It would appear that the system perceives a greater degree of control over health care workers who are salaried employees. Nurses like other large employee groups have felt the need to seek the protection and security of unionization. Doctors are becoming organized as well. Administrative personnel gain their protection and security both from a position of control and also from written policies and procedures (processes). As long as procedures are followed, as with any other committee no one individual can be faulted.

The role of doctors and their attitude has been undergoing continuous change for years. They are now inclined to retire early, not to accept calls after hours, to take more days off, not to work nights or weekends, and to give up their hospital privileges altogether. It seems they have evolved from the traditional patient-loyal, house-call-making, family doctor who delivered and cared for his 'flock' from birth to death. Their orientation has moved more toward self and 'à la carte' care. One new model has physicians employed by hospitals and clinics, no longer self-employed entrepreneurs. The impact of their transformation from that of the independent businessperson into a company-loyal salaried person has yet to be felt by most patients. Has their attitude changed? You be the judge. Can we blame them? The self employed ones who are left behind now have a variety of controls on their income and practice patterns (e.g. salary caps which limits the number of patients they see). Do you think this environment fosters strong patient loyalty? Remember, this trend is only just beginning; imagine the impact of young nurses and doctors growing up in this environment. To them the non-patient centred universe is the 'norm'. Everybody cares, from 9 to 5!

Then too, patients' attitudes are not helping; nor does the system encourage them to help. Many patients feel that because they have prepaid for their care (through taxes, etc.) they will use it as often as they wish. From the necessary to the most unnecessary (to the downright ridiculous) complaints, patients are bringing everything to their overburdened physicians. Does every cough, cold, flu, cut, and ache have to be seen? Why are there so many repeated visits for the same complaint and the same advice? Is this the patient demanding care? Some would argue the doctor is looking for business. The doctor doesn't need the business!

We are using the system more. Our attitudes are changing. We should not have to wait. We deserve the newest and the most expensive technology and medication. Any doctor will do (who cares about a relationship?). We have not meaningfully participated. We are more than willing to sue if not satisfied. This is a sure-fire recipe for disaster. In short we are at war with our own health care system! It is time to re-examine our attitudes (yes - all of us), and begin to look for ways to pull together, rather than create bigger divides between patients, doctors, and the health care system. It is already suffering from extensive fragmentation.

"Patients die needlessly, says [Dr. John] Millar, because health care is run like a cottage industry: a number of dispersed individual operators with minimal electronic sharing of information"

Danylo Hawaleshka
Maclean's · December, 2002

★ ★ ★ ★ ★

Fragmentation

In general, patients are overwhelmed and under-prepared when they get sick. Whether in an accident or dealing with a chronic disease such as diabetes, patients usually sit back and watch the events around them unfold. Often people are caught speechless or fumbling for an answer when a doctor asks them for information regarding their complaint. They have not thought through their symptoms, nor have they recorded any information about how bad or how often their symptoms are occurring. In other words, they are watching the game, not playing.

Is it the *"I have no control"* or "I *don't know how to participate"* patient strategy that forces health care professionals to take over? Or, as many believe, is it the health care professionals who created and perpetuate the subservient patient from their lofty positions of power and authority? Most people are all too happy to simply hand over the responsibility for the outcome of their problem. If it works, great. If it doesn't, someone is at fault! Very few actively participate in the important decisions regarding their health care. Why? There is more easily accessible information today than ever before in history. Patients want, want, want. But do they know exactly *what* they want? Patients are afraid today. They are in a prepaid system but there are line-ups for everything. Their doctor is unavailable, they have no doctor, it's after hours so they have to go to someone else, and their health records are scattered about. If they complain too much, they may not have a doctor and they could lose their place in line. Any human being put in a position of insecurity will solve that problem in the safest, quickest way possible. In the health care universe (with few options available), patients orbit (like planets) seeking help for their problems. What are they really looking for? They are looking for history; they are looking for what they used to have, a doctor who cares, is available, willing to talk and to educate them.

In the past, doctors were equipped with a broader perspective and a deeper working knowledge of their patients. Knowing the patient's history was an integral part of the caring process. Now it appears that doctors are incredibly focused (super specialized), and deal primarily with medical 'incidents'. They no longer deal with the patient's overall 'health life'. In fact, they often do not have a complete patient's medical record, let alone an appreciation of them as *unique individuals.* You can see how it is increasingly important that patients take responsibility for their personal health care records.

Also in the past, doctors had a great deal of time to spend building trust and solid relationships with their patients. The illnesses they treated were not life-long but brief episodes that they either cured or could not. Their knowledge was limited in comparison to today and they did what they could by attempting to understand their patient's problems. Now, we have the knowledge to treat many diseases, but doctors have less time to communicate. The paradox is that doctors are dealing with more and more complicated, chronic patients who need extra time, but who are unfortunately getting less.

Because of specialization and changes in practice patterns patients now see many different physicians at different times, in different locations and for different reasons. Your health care record consists of a series of physician and institutional files, each of which is incomplete. For example your cardiologist may interview you and come to a diagnosis and treatment plan. If you require an angiogram, it may be done by another cardiologist who performs that particular test. If you then require a balloon angioplasty or coronary bypass, it will be done by another heart specialist. Your recovery may be supervised by yet another heart specialist. Fragmentation!

Be aware: the communication between these physicians is less than adequate.

On the surface, it may seem that the patient is getting more attention. What is really happening is that their individual complaints and illnesses are being attended to but the patient is becoming increasingly anonymous, perhaps the worst thing that can happen. We run the risk of having treatment errors, visits repeated, no follow-up plans, misdiagnosis, improper treatment strategies and dangerous combinations of drugs. This lack of a committed professional relationship, fragmented files and overall anonymity undermines your ability to be a Priority Patient! You can be forgotten! NEXT!

Keys To Living Without A Doctor

Very few people get through life without requiring the services of a physician. It is not impossible to live without a personal physician but it can be difficult and may be dangerous. If you find yourself in this situation, don't panic! You must believe you are smart enough to do what needs to be done. Have faith in yourself and be confident. It won't necessarily be easy, and you will periodically require professional medical advice. This implies that you are taking charge. You must pay attention and learn as much as you can about your particular situation and individual health care needs. You are following advice that has been given to you previously. You can actually develop a great deal of expertise in dealing with your particular problem simply by remembering all of the medical advice you have been given and complementing this with additional education and personal research.

Remember most of the time you are not with your doctor. *You* deal with *your* symptoms and *your* medical problems on a day-to-day basis. Nobody sees their doctor every day. Think about it; even if you are fortunate enough to have a personal physician, you probably only see him two or three times a year. The rest of the time you're in charge, you are living without a doctor. It is only when something occurs with which you are unfamiliar that you may seek the advice of a physician or other medical professional. Now you realize how important it is to listen, understand and record *all* of the advice that you are given, since you base your self-care on this information. A good doctor will help you.

Actions To Take When Your Doctor Is Leaving/Closing The Practice

It is never easy when a physician leaves the community. Every community is different. Patients can be left with a sense of abandonment and confusion. More important is the fact that they are left with the enormous task of handling their own health matters. They more than likely have no personal medical file. They should! These days, it is unlikely that the departing physician found a replacement to take over his practice. It is indeed a daunting (often impossible) task to find a new doctor. If you had an excellent doctor/patient relationship, you will indeed be saddened when your physician partner departs since replacing this relationship is a most difficult challenge. Finding another doctor for a temporary problem is relatively easy; walk-in, after-hours clinic, ER, etc. If you're ready for the challenge, read on and good luck!

Set up a final appointment so that you can ask your current physician at least the following questions *before* his departure. You probably won't get another chance!

Questions To Ask Before Your Doctor Leaves

- Where will your records be stored?
- How can you access them if necessary?
- Can you have a copy of your records?
- Is there a fee for obtaining your records?
- Is the practice being taken over by a new doctor?
- What plan is in place for transferring your records
- to a new doctor?
- If the office is downsizing, will you be one of the patients they keep?
- Will your doctor be returning?
- Can your file copy include test results and specialist consultations?
- Can your doctor give you a summary of recommendations regarding your ongoing care?

Avoiding The Care-Gap

If you really want to aim for a smooth transition and give yourself more time to secure a new physician there are more important strategies that can certainly facilitate the changes that are about to occur. Don't get caught in a care-gap!

Strategies For Avoiding The Care-Gap

- Ask for as many repeats on prescription medications as possible.
- Try to get a 2 or month prescription with at least 6 repeats.
- Keep a photocopy of the prescription.
- Send your doctor a thank you card (you're losing a friend)!
- Get a personalized reference letter to a specialist if necessary, just in case they try to book an appointment for you and it gets cancelled after your doctor's office is already closed. This may leave you hunting for a new referral or booking.
- Ask your doctor for a strategy to deal with medical problems that may occur before you find a replacement (e.g. local nurse practitioner or local medical society, etc.).
- Ask any other important questions that pertain to you and your particular situation at the time. This is your last chance!

Actions To Take When You Realize You No Longer Have A Personal Physician

The first and most important thing to do is to create or purchase your own personal health care diary. You will not succeed at managing your own health care if you do not maintain complete and accurate records. You need to be able to convey to your replacement physician the history of your medical problems and details regarding treatment you have received and how you have responded. Extremely important here are issues such as life threatening allergies, advance directives, serious surgical events, past and current medications, medication reactions and prosthetic devices (artificial parts). If you create and maintain your own medical record, you will understand your health situation and you will be less likely to allow mistakes to occur. You are well on your way to becoming a Priority Patient! Start by getting copies of your previous medical records.

Trace Your Records (there will be a cost)

- Call your former doctor's office old phone number.
- Call your doctor's former clinic manager.
- Call local medical records storage facilities.
- Contact your former doctor's website.
- Call your doctor's new office.
- Call the medical records department at the hospital you have attended.
- Call all previous physicians, clinics and hospital medical records departments that you have attended.
- Call the local provincial medical association to inquire if your former doctor has left any forwarding instructions.

There are a couple of other tips for those who really want to be successful at ensuring continuity. If possible, it's wise to pick up your records in person! - Make sure they are *yours* and they are complete. Next, consult your other physicians! – If you already have a specialist you may want to discuss the following issues:

Questions To Ask Your Other Physicians

- Are you allowed to arrange a follow-up appointment yourself?
- Will they renew your prescriptions until you find a new doctor?
- Can they recommend a new personal physician for you?
- Can you rely on them to continue to treat your specific problem?
- If not, can you have a copy of your files?
- Do they have any specific advice for you now that they realize you are on your own with a problem that requires a specialist?

The Search Begins!

Finding a new doctor could take months. There is a critical shortage of personal physicians at this time. This will continue for years. The impact of this shortage in part depends on your location. All communities are searching for physicians. You may get lucky and find a new doctor very quickly. Good luck! Others may have to search for months to even get in to see a doctor to discuss the matter. There are many places you can look for a new physician with whom to build a new relationship.

Places To Find A New Doctor

- Ask your current doctor – do they have a replacement?
- Ask your specialist – do they know of a replacement?
- Ask your pharmacist.
- Attend a local walk-in clinic. Some will take on permanent patients.
- Check the phone book.
- Call the local medical association.
- Call the provincial medical society.
- Call the college of physicians and surgeons.
- Consult with your company's medical department.
- Ask family members and friends about access to their doctors.
- Check with local hospital medical departments.
- Call your local MP or the Mayor's office.

Many large cities even have a directory or contact line that you can phone, and they will recommend someone. In some communities there are now nurse practitioners available. Don't wait until you are sick to try to find a doctor! Once you are sick it is a little late to be selective. In the emergency room or walk-in clinic you take the doctor on call. You are anonymous and treated like a number. There is no relationship! Welcome stranger!

Information and preparation will once again be your salvation. If you are able, find out everything possible about your medical condition(s). You may even want to turn to the Internet if necessary. Keep helpful websites listed in your 'favourites', and get all possible pamphlets with facts regarding your illness.

Living With Or Without A Doctor

Regardless of your current health care situation, you need to understand that the majority of the time you are on your own. Health care professionals are available when you need them. They come and go. Most of their offices are open 9 to 5, Monday to Friday. Whether or not you have a personal physician they are seldom available to you on weekends or holidays. If you suddenly get sick and call your doctor you will likely be directed to go to the emergency department anyway. When was the last time you had a house call?

The following tactics will assist you in managing your health life. They are not designed to replace a physician. They are presented to you as techniques to encourage your development as a Priority Patient and give you a new, more self-confident frame of mind. There are 24 hours in a day, 365 days in a year and your last appointment with the doctor was completed in 10 minutes. Even the specialist spends less than an hour with you. You spend far more time with yourself!

Survival Tactic #1 - *Learn To Assess & Record Your Symptoms*

- Does your symptom need attention now, tomorrow or next week?
- What makes you think it requires a doctor?
- What would you expect of a doctor?
- Frequency, severity, location, relievers, aggravators
- When did it start?
- Have you had it before?
- What helps to relieve it?
- Is it mild, moderate, or severe?

The Priority Patient is able to record and communicate details of their symptoms. As untrained observers, patients frequently make errors in judgment as to the seriousness of their symptoms. This is not unexpected. However if you have recorded and learned from your mistakes, your errors will decrease.

Survival Tactic #2 - *Keep In Touch With Your Body*

- Know your dietary habits, average calories, and type of foods that you should eat.
- Maintain an exercise program.
- Keep track of and try to stay at a healthy weight.
- Note any unexpected changes (change in bowel movements, type, frequency, etc.)
- Observe changes in your usual complexion and colouring.
- Watch for signs of abnormality (such as burning when you urinate, etc.)
- Keep track of regular symptoms like headaches.

The Priority Patient maintains a healthy lifestyle, and recognizes unexplained changes in body appearance and function. Minor complaints are evaluated and recorded.

Survival Tactic #3 - *Respond To Your Body*

Watch for:

- Unexplained weight loss
- Bleeding
- Yellow or green sputum
- Black bowel movements
- Persistent diarrhea/constipation
- Double vision
- Persistent headaches, dizziness, numbness (especially after hitting your head)
- Unexplained chest discomfort
- Yellow eyes
- A changing mole on your skin

The Priority Patient does not hesitate to act; significant alterations are not ignored but are recorded and brought to the attention of a health care professional.

Survival Tactic #4 - *Get Educated Wherever You Can*

- Your pharmacist (regarding medication, doses, timing, etc.)
- Magazine articles on wellness or specific diseases
- Library books on health and disease
- Community resources
- Science clubs and guest speakers
- Professional association websites
- Individual PHYSICIAN websites (not fly-by-night product web pages)
- Hospital websites

The Priority Patient makes herself aware of the many sources of health care information not only in their local community but also in various media outlets. She also focuses on specific information pertaining to her individual health care concerns.

Survival Tactic #5 - *Learn To Monitor & Record*

- Blood pressure - Record your BP.
- Sugar diabetes - Record sugar levels and medication doses.
- Blood thinners - Record blood test results and medication doses.
- Body weight - Weekly
- Fluid balance -Some diseases demand limited fluid consumption.
- Side effects of medication - Record as you would any symptom and include how long after your medication they occur.
- Reactions to medications in general – Even over the counter drugs

The Priority Patient is aware of the complexities of self-care and makes herself able to measure and monitor various indicators of health and disease. The patient with high blood pressure MUST be able to measure their blood pressure. A Priority Patient knows their medications and would NEVER take a medication that they had previously had a bad reaction to.

Survival Tactic #6 - *Use Other Professional Services & Clubs*

- Pharmacy information centres
- Blood pressure clinics
- Diabetic education lectures
- Breast screening forums
- Interest groups with invited lecturers
- YMCA/YWCA information programs
- Medical professional community presentations

The Priority Patient takes advantage of any and all opportunities to learn from experts, particularly in fields that pertain to her individual health interests. Often she will question the experts directly.

Survival Tactic #7 - *Neighbourhood Health Clubs*

- Form a club with friends and neighbours to meet regularly and learn from the way others manage their health issues.
- Web chats - There are many message boards dedicated to every illness and symptom.
- Send a representative from your health club to clinics, hospitals, and government facilities to learn about existing support services, programs and facilities.
- If you have a specific chronic illness there are often support groups.

The Priority Patient initiates information groups and seeks out others with similar health concerns to create networks for sharing health information and resources.

Survival Tactic #8 - *Walk-In Clinics/ ERs/ Nurse Practitioners*

- Find out when the doctor you saw last will be working again.
- Make note of the doctor's name.
- Keep records of diagnosis and treatment.
- Try to make an appointment with the doctor's personal office for follow-up (hopefully as a new patient).
- Always take your health care diary.
- Ensure that management of the current problem

The Priority Patient is treated as a complete individual not just as a disease or complaint. All efforts are made to see the same professional each time. A complete health care diary includes records from all sources.

Survival Tactic #9 - *Volunteer For A Research Trial*

- You are guaranteed to see a physician if you participate.
- Know what the risks and benefits are to you.
- Certain tests are done to monitor your kidney, liver, blood count, urinalysis, ECG or x-rays.
- Ask for a complete summary of your participation and results.
- Keep copies of all the results in your health care diary as they may be needed later for something unrelated.

The Priority Patient understands the importance of research and the benefits to patient participants. The investigators are usually high quality health care professionals and can offer advice on issues such as finding a physician.

Chapter Summary

☞ **Don't wait until you are in trouble to find a replacement!**

☞ **Keep in touch with your body.**

☞ **Create and use a personal health care diary!**

☞ **Keep your own records accurate and up to date.**

☞ **Be practical, maximize every health care encounter.**

☞ **Think ahead – prescriptions, advice, etc.**

☞ **Don't be afraid of having to live without a personal doctor.**

☞ **Learn everything you can about *you*!**

☞ **Use all resources that are available to you.**

☞ **It is your health – GET INVOLVED!!**

Secrets Of Physician Variability

No, doctors are not all the same. Most of us are confused when one doctor suggests a treatment that is not recommended by another. You should recognize that there are usually several treatments to choose from that are suitable for any particular medical problem. Just as there are many choices in health care, there is significant variability amongst physicians. Patients tend to think of medical professionals as members of a unified group all of whom have the same background, training, and experience. While doctors do have a particular 'belief system' (similar way of perceiving people and situations), they are also individuals.

People tend to believe that medicine is an exact science. When two physicians differ, patients question which of the two is wrong. The fact is they may both be *right*. Doctors are human and vary as much as any other group of creative professionals. In fact, a doctor may not choose the same treatment each time they are faced with a patient presenting with the same problem. This change in approach is seen not only from patient to patient but also from time to time. It likely reflects a 'customized approach' to individual patients. It also may indicate an evolution of knowledge and skill. In fact, one should be concerned if such changes are not obvious over time. For example, one particular doctor may consistently favour a certain approach no matter what! Doctors are individuals and practicing medicine is an art.

Why Are Doctors Different?

Professionally, doctors are not usually differentiated by their personality, character, bedside manner, religious beliefs or marital status. Their selection for educational programs, hospital privileges, employment opportunities, etc., is based on their professional credentials and whether or not they have any official complaints registered against them. Like other professionals, they originate from a wide range of backgrounds and are influenced by lifestyle demands. Patients seldom consider these non-professional aspects. While the health care system is supposed to be non-biased and impartial (much like our judicial system), it is naive to believe that physicians are impartial and bias-free. All of us are raised with beliefs that guide our decision-making, relationships with others and the way we conduct our business. These are subconscious rules that we follow every day. They are part of the belief system that we were taught. For example, when we were little we were taught to be polite and have manners, to be fair and not to steal. Our daily actions reflect our upbringing and our experiences. It is no wonder that doctors are not simple carbon copies of one another; they are only human!

What Doctors Do Differently

The answer is simple. Everything!

- They have vastly different bedside manners.
- They have different opinions.
- Some use diagnostic tests more frequently.
- Some are more available.
- They diagnose and prescribe differently.
- They interpret research results and published data differently.
- They use the results of positive and negative tests differently.
- Some are naturally more aggressive than others.
- Some appear more dedicated.
- Some are more academic.

Did you know that if we were to ask three physicians to interpret any particular diagnostic test, two would agree on the result and the other would disagree most of the time. It is also true that in the process of analysing test results, the same physician will disagree with his own interpretation (at another time) about 20-30% of the time! In other words, the result of a test *is* the interpretation. Interpretations vary! Such things as fatigue, expertise, training, interruption, and technical quality of the test and patient factors can have important influence on test interpretation.

Why They Do It Differently

One of the most important reasons why doctors behave differently in apparently similar situations is the patient. If you think about it, until the patient arrives and describes her problem, there is no contact. What the doctor does in essence, is react to the patient's presentation. *You* initiate the situation; *you* are the trigger for what happens next. In this context 'you' are two things; the person and the symptom. Any symptom or complaint can be presented in a variety of ways.

Symptoms can be *minimized* or *dramatized*. To a large extent the presentation is decided by the individual patient and their personality. If a patient enters the doctor's examining room hunched over and complaining of "unbearable" abdominal pain, things will be perceived as urgent. If on the other hand, the patient walks in with the same level of pain and describes it as a "sore stomach", the doctor will show less immediate concern.

The doctor, observing the patient's behaviour, *reacts* and begins the process of problem solving in a time frame that reflects the specific patient's presentation. You can appreciate the tremendous potential for variation. Some physicians are thorough in extracting information from their patients (the history) before the physical examination begins; almost an inquisition. They probe for details many of which may seem irrelevant. But are they really? A good patient history is the key to as much as 75% of the diagnosis. Some doctors however appear too busy for a lengthy history or discussion. They appear inattentive, or worse, may ask the patient to be quiet! You may well improve your doctor's problem-solving accuracy by presenting the problem in detail. Some physicians may react more to the patient, some to the problem, and many to the way the problem is presented.

Types Of Doctors

Doctors come in all shapes and sizes and other descriptors. Some you like and some you don't. Some are family practitioners and some are specialists. Some look after you like you are a precious jewel, while others practice piecework. Some seem to have all day to talk, some have only minutes. Some are thorough some are not. Some seem vastly more intelligent than others. Some act like a member of your family while others act like strangers. Some have better reputations than others. Is this real, or is it all appearances and hearsay?

You don't really know, do you? Until you build a meaningful doctor/patient partnership and both of you understand and appreciate the other, you don't know. You are guessing. You are hoping. In today's fragmented health care system, a doc is a doc is a doc! Any doctor will do! Most judgments are based on appearances. For example doctors are described as:

- Very busy, having no time
- Being abrupt, cold
- Inattentive
- Friendly, kind, caring
- Intelligent, brilliant
- Pompous, self important, arrogant
- Fatherly/motherly
- Etc.

What is the patient describing? Is the patient considering the doctor's expertise or knowledge? Are they simply measuring his bedside manner, reputation or character? Although a doctor may be friendly and *appear* to be good at what he does, this does not ensure that he is! Likewise the most brilliant physician in the world can be socially inept and unable to handle patient communication. It's the same as describing an acquaintance or your very best friend.

What's Your Doctor's Alias?

Doctors sometimes fit the stereotypes....

These names are for fun and by no means reflect any actual individuals

A doctor with a lot of wisdom .... Dr. Wise-man
A pompous, self- important Doctor .... Dr. R. O. Gant
A doctor who wants his own way...................... Dr. O. VerBearing
A doctor who uses no intuition or thought......... Dr. R. E. Flex
A caring and compassionate doctor .... Dr. M. Pathetic
A doctor with very little time............................ Dr. Vair E. Busy
A doctor that's always rushing to the next patient. Dr. Ena Hurry
A doctor with an excellent bedside manner....... Dr. Hans Holder

What's Your Nurse's Alias?

Nurses can have typical personalities too....

These names are for fun and by no means reflect any actual individuals

The nurse who is always in charge..................... Nurse Major
The nurse who pays strict attention to detail...... Nurse Tek Nickle
The compassionate nurse............................... Nurse Kare Ing
The nurse who needs to retire.......................... Nurse Mean Nold
The nurse who is over-worked.......................... Nurse Ima Busy
The nurse with a lot of knowledge and skill........ Nurse Almos Adoc
The nurse who does not want to deal with you.... Nurse Wa Chawant
The nurse who won't bend the rules.................. Nurse Bytha Book

Common Qualities

Some desirable qualities your physician may possess are obvious. Pick from this list what your doctor has and what you would like him to have.

> personality, experience, maturity, individuality, skills, bias
> independence, commitment, happiness, desire, integrity
> principles, interest, adaptability, creativity, insight, focus
> involvement, knowledge, habits, wisdom, security, honesty

Can you imagine trying to do this with a perfect stranger seen once at a health care outlet, especially when you are sick?

Patients should look beyond their physician's appearance and mannerisms. Try to recognize wisdom in your personal physician. This is not an easy task. Just remember, it has been said "There is a dramatic difference between 20 years of experience and one year's experience repeated 20 times". Try to choose a physician who appears to learn from his experiences and does not simply work on autopilot or by an algorithm-based philosophy. Some patients prefer younger physicians because they see them as having the newest knowledge, while others take comfort in years of experience and the wisdom of age. If you prefer 'à la carte' medical care, this may not be an issue for you. However if you want continuity of care from your personal physician, you must connect! Know your doctor as they must know you!

What You May Not Know About Your Doctor....

Like the rest of us, doctors have good days and bad days. Like other self-regulating groups, the responsibility for good practice, ethical behaviour, and high standards, sits with the individual professional and the regulating bodies. Much of the responsibility is on the shoulders of the individual physician. Your doctor's decision making may be influenced by a purely scientific background since a broad-based (liberal arts) education is not a prerequisite for medical school.

Performance evaluations are unusual in the medical profession. Critical analysis of the literature seems far more common than self-criticism. If your doctor practices for many years without a performance evaluation (which may very well reveal errors and inconsistencies) he may eventually assume that he can do no wrong! When was the last time you asked for a background check on the physician making important treatment decisions on your behalf?

Playing Both Roles

Elsewhere in this book (The Doctor's World) it is pointed out that physicians play a number of roles in society, all of which can profoundly affect their variability. Another important reason why physicians are so variable is that they are torn between two opposing professional and social roles. On one hand, they are the *patient's advocate* and their primary focus must be patient care. Simultaneously, they are the gatekeepers of society's health care system, and are forced to consider such issues as funding and resource utilization in this role as 'responsible corporate citizen'. Thus, their decisions can be variably affected by medical and corporate pressures. Some doctors could care less what a pacemaker costs! The process of integrating these roles affects *every* decision.

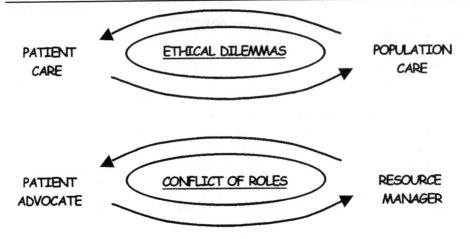

Physicians Are Variable So Buyer Beware!

Knowing this, all that can be said is 'buyer beware'. You will receive the level of health care that you accept. If you observe carefully your doctor's approach to you, you may just find a physician that has all of the qualities that you need to feel confident and secure. It is after all your health. You have to trust the physician you choose and be comfortable with the choices that you make together.

Chapter Summary

- **Doctors are different from each other!**

- **It takes work to find the doctor best suited to you.**

- **Medical decisions are based on more than disease!**

- **Treatments vary from person to person, time to time.**

- **Some doctors are smarter than others.**

- **Test results are subject to interpretation doctors interpret.**

- **Doctors play societal roles that affect decision-making.**

- **Physicians are just people.**

Keys To Dealing With Health Care Professionals and Support Staff

Doctors, nurses and secretaries are some of the people you will meet during your illness. These are people you need and they are within reach. They are not legislators, regulators or administrators or absentee landlords. Their main objective is to help you. In busy health care outlets such as hospital emergency rooms, doctors and nurses provide care, in a fast-paced, high-pressure, 'efficient' environment. The pressures created by financial restrictions, tight budgets, institutional policies and contemporary efficiencies as well as the need to meet professional standards all have a significant impact on delivery of care. They 'process' as many patients as possible in the time available. The front door never or rarely closes! The picture resembles the floor of a busy stock exchange in a tumultuous market.

Getting Noticed

To the medical and nursing staff in the emergency room, the patient always comes first. That fact may not be immediately obvious. Processing and caring for patients may or may not be the same thing. While they are concerned about each patient, they know that patients must be processed in a reasonable period of time. There are times when the pressures of the environment may have undue influence over the appearance of care. Although it may appear that you are being treated in an abrupt or impersonal fashion, don't assume this indicates lack of concern. This environment frequently creates tension among patients and professionals. Priority Patients recognize those times and situations in which health care professionals require a great deal of understanding and patience.

It would not be prudent to advise anyone to jump up and down and scream *"I'm what's important!!"* or *"I'm the patient, I come first!!"* That type of behaviour not only is ineffective, but counterproductive! Remember you are in a line up and they are doing the best they can. In these difficult situations, good manners are very effective tools. While this might sound ridiculous at first, an unbelievable amount of progress can be made by simply being *nice*. This does not mean that you should not insist on good care. It does mean that you may not always get exactly what you want; it may be beyond the individual's ability to offer it. Using good manners will generally get you through the system quicker and with fewer obstacles. An aggressive approach. You will get attention but not better care! Although other environments may be less tense, the basic rules still apply.

Being Clear While Being Firm

As in any other business in which human beings interact, there are strategies that you as a patient should consider when dealing with others. Try using a friendly, talkative, cooperative and easy-going style. At the same time you need to appear serious, informed, resolved and very clear about your personal concerns. Be considerate of the fact that most health care personnel and their staff are busy. Personalize the encounter if possible, by saying things like *"How are you today, Mary?"* or *"Doctor Jones, it's always a pleasure to see you"*. The greeting sets the mood for the rest of the encounter. However, don't be a fake. Remember, on another day, they might be the patient. So be sincere, be friendly and be you.

Understand The People With Whom You Are Dealing

Medical support staff and even some doctors assume that patients are all the same. Likewise, patients assume that doctors, nurses and secretaries are all the same; nameless, faceless processors! Unfortunately, this is the biggest mistake you can make. Every professional is an *individual.* Every medical office has it's own personality. Doctors and their support staff are not governed by one large anonymous organization that tells them how to behave. Don't assume that every office is the same. It is extremely helpful that you recognize the type of people you are dealing with and adjust your approach accordingly.

Personality Types To Watch For

Your approach to each type of physician, nurse and secretary is important in order to maximize your level of priority and the time they make available to you. Consider the style of physicians you have met before as you read the following. Each patient has to decide what they want and what they can get from a particular physician. Patients should optimize their medical encounters by recognizing what they need to do to be considered Priority Patients.

Some doctors approach their patients as intelligent, informed and concerned about their health. They will usually outline the various options available to the patient, perhaps recommend the preferred strategy and then expect the patient to make the final decision. This can be intimidating to patients who feel less than confident in their ability to handle their specific health issues. However, this type of physician encourages a greater amount of involvement and expects active patient participation. This type of physician knows that it is your health and not theirs that is at stake.

Some of these physician types are more informal in their approach to patients. It would not be unusual to see humour used frequently in this type of relationship. This is an excellent environment for communication. Time and efficiency issues will be of secondary importance to this type of physician.

Another type of physician may not be as approachable, but still leaves room for a comfortable level of communication. This doctor generally presents treatment options to the patient and suggests his preferred choice. This is not always accompanied by a clear explanation, but he does not hesitate to explain when asked. This doctor is somewhat more formal, but the patient can establish a better level of communication by doing simple things such as making eye contact, and simply requesting more information. It is important to let this type of physician know that you value their opinion but you still want to know all of your options.

Another category of physician is either more difficult or easier to deal with depending on the type of patient you are. He simply tells patients exactly what to do, no questions, no joint decisions. He merely wants the patient to listen and comply. Patient participation is neither requested nor desired. You have likely met one of them before. He can present a problem for the patient who is trying to stay in charge of her own health. These physicians often say they don't have time to answer questions or explain the reasons for their decisions. Although you may be comforted by having decisions made for you, lack of participation on your part does not absolve you from sharing responsibility for the outcome.

Physicians in General

Doctors and their practices can be as different as night and day. Their size, shape and personalities are as varied as any other group of human beings. Their mission in life however, is the care of their patients. When interacting with physicians, patients should remember a few general rules regarding communication.

Communication Skills

- Be concise – explain your symptoms clearly.
- Don't be intimidated – ask all of your questions.
- Be friendly and polite.
- Express your gratitude.
- Develop trust and loyalty with your doctor.
- Make a treatment plan with your doctor and STICK TO IT!

Don't forget, the physician wants to help his patient. If you fail to cooperate in your care, expect to be treated differently. Priority Patients educate, participate and cooperate.

Nurses

Patients are often unaware of the specific role nurses play in their health care. Local circumstances dictate the amount of responsibility nurses are given. Their training and capabilities can vary widely. In some situations they may assist in the process of diagnosis and even treatment. In other situations they may be delegated routine tasks such as measurement of blood pressure and temperature. In large hospitals many nurses occupy roles in the management structure. In the past, nurses were unfortunately treated as the doctor's helper. Today, they have an increasingly independent role in the health care system; individually and as a group. In some jurisdictions the level of education required is a university degree. Some generate original research particularly in the areas of communication, compassion and human caring.

It is easy to see why patients have difficulty deciding where the nurse fits in the overall scheme of their medical care. This will be dictated by circumstance and location. In a doctor's office or walk-in clinic the nurse has a very specific role that is quickly obvious. In a hospital setting there are many different roles dictated by circumstances. The nurse may be directly involved in your immediate care, more senior and in charge of the unit, on an audit or research project acquiring data, or be an administrative director of a hospital program. Your primary contact in the hospital will be with the nurses directly involved in your immediate care. Treat them well and understand that if anyone in the business of medicine is extremely busy, it's the nurse!

Nurses Are Limited By:

- **Time available** -
  They often have many patients at one time.
- **Regulations and standards**-
  Their actions are heavily controlled.
- **Professional training** –
  They have limits to what they can do for patients.
- **Legal issues** –
  There are heavy legal penalties for errors.
- **Protocols and Algorithms** –
  They must follow established guidelines.
- **Doctor's Orders** –
  They are obliged to follow these (except in extreme circumstances).

Priority Patients are aware that the doctor may only see them for five minutes per day in the hospital, but the nurse looks after them for a twelve-hour shift. Nurses tolerate the bulk of the burden of patient discontent. If a patient is going to act out it is usually directed at the nurse not the physician. Priority Patients treat their nurse with the same degree of respect and understanding as they do their physician! While there may be relatively little nursing input into the medical decision making process, your daily contact and level of comfort in hospital is established by your relationship with the nurse.

Secretaries And Support Staff

Believe it or not, these people practice their own art form. Booking appointments, arranging diagnostic tests and deciding if you need to be seen today or next month requires certain skill. Much of it is common sense but a great deal of it is knowing the patients and the workings of the system. These activities are stressful and hectic. At the beginning of every encounter, clearly identify yourself. Be brief and to the point. The details are for the doctor. Priority Patients are patient! When you arrive at the office, be prepared with your health registration information and be on time! Try to follow instructions carefully. Be prepared to wait!

Priority Patients give office personnel the respect they deserve and are rewarded. Office personnel appreciate it when you make your wants and needs clearly understood. They also appreciate it when you understand the limitations of the system. Don't shoot the messenger! However, if you feel you have been treated poorly look for a comment card or inform your physician. If you repeatedly question the way you are treated, understand that office atmosphere is largely set by the physician. Particularly when dealing with medical office or clinic staff, understand the inherent flexibility in their position and recognize that they can respond to the individual patient's needs if they are clearly identified. Priority Patients can sometimes be accommodated when others can't. There will be many times when your request is not possible. A good secretary will try to find you a suitable alternative.

★ ★ ★ ★ ★

"Being sensitive to the doctor's [or office staff's] time constraints and pressure is another example of how the two-way street makes things work better....Basic human-to-human honesty can go a long way"

Dr. Peeter Poldre

Toronto Star · November, 2002

Chapter Summary

- Professionals are people too (and they can easily have very bad days).

- Office staff are people too!

- Don't be afraid to express your gratitude.

- Remember that manners are the key.

- Establish a good rapport with your health care team.

- Ensure that you communicate your needs clearly.

Secrets Of The Doctor's World

It is important to appreciate that the decision making process is not taken lightly by physicians. They spend years learning the art of diagnosis. They pride themselves on being right, so it is difficult to let patients in on this process especially if the patient does not appear to be particularly prepared or confident about the role they play. How could patients possibly comprehend something that took the doctor over ten years to perfect. Most doctors make a thousand decisions a day!

Medicine is a shared responsibility. It is this aspect of health and wellness that frightens people. They prefer to believe that the doctor is all knowing and does not make mistakes. To realize that doctors are human beings and the profession of medicine is like any other job is like discovering there is no Santa Clause. Some people blindly believe that all patients receive generic, gold-star, 'evidence-based' treatment, including the newest and best 'state-of-the-art' technology known to mankind. Actually, what they are getting is the best treatment and newest technology known to that particular physician. Guess what, not all doctors got 80% in medical school, and not all doctors are up to date with the new knowledge! As in any other profession, medicine has its superstars as well as its below average players.

Traditional Training

Training to become a physician is a long and arduous task. Medical students must undergo a rigorous and lengthy training process that can strip away their original sense of self and remould them into society's *ideal* physician. This sets the stage for their viewing the human body as a diseased machine, thus allowing them to tolerate their continuous exposure to the pain of human suffering. This training can be described as intense, demanding, competitive, and most of all exhausting. Recovering from this dehumanizing process (if ever) may require many years of clinical practice to appreciate that their patients are people not just diseases. Medical school assures society that all of its graduates are well versed in the knowledge of diseases and their treatments. It is an illusion to assume that they are all able to communicate beyond the level of the science of disease. Wisdom takes time and experience!

Everyone Must Play By The Rules!

Doctors have a unique set of rules for behaviour that are deep-rooted and go back to their training. These rules of behaviour are necessary to ensure that they function successfully. Although likely unaware of these cultural behaviours, they are perpetuated by the schooling process. Doctors train doctors to be doctors! These same unwritten rules, which have held true for so many years, have allowed for a predictable pattern of health care delivery. For example, one of these unwritten rules is that doctors approach the human body as a mechanical device with individual parts. They look at patients as having pieces that need to be fixed (or God forbid - replaced). A doctor's approach to the human body is based on a need to identify and cure disease, an unshakeable self-confidence and a profound sense of responsibility.

What Drives Your Doctor

To understand your doctor (and better communicate with him), there are a few things you need to know. Why is your doctor so self-confident (some to the point of arrogance)? Why does he act like an authority figure? Why can't he admit when he is wrong? Why does he use words you can't understand? Why does he withhold the biological details of your problems? When was the last time he had an annual performance appraisal?

Doctors gain unique expertise in medical school which leads to self-confidence and a sense of authority (even superiority?). One bi-product of this process can be difficulty communicating verbally and emotionally with their patients. It frequently appears that all doctors are consumed with prescribing medication, ordering diagnostic tests, and 'curing' patients. With all of the new technology at their disposal, some doctors seem to be losing touch with the compassionate side of medicine. It is often easier in this fast-paced world to *act* rather than *communicate*.

The emphasis has changed from a good doctor/patient relationship to a 'quick fix' approach. The total patient (holistic) approach of the past has surrendered to the any doctor will do, walk-in, complaint focused style of health care delivery that we have today. The only thing that's missing is a drive-through window. That may be coming! Disease-oriented practitioners love the algorithmic, piecework style of medicine that enables them to avoid challenging human interactions.

Spending Quality Time With Patients

It was once believed that a good patient history was adequate to make the diagnosis 75% of the time. However, that was when diagnoses were simple! Today we seek more detailed and complex diagnoses, the descriptions of which cannot be obtained from the patient. In the pursuit of more quantitative scientific information about disease processes, we have sacrificed much of the critically important, albeit subjective information easily obtainable from the patient if time allows. Instead, we get answers from (and worship?) increasingly complex and expensive, occasionally risky diagnostic testing. Diagnostic tests should be used to confirm a diagnosis obtained by a thorough history-taking process; doctor and patient interacting and becoming aware of each other.

The patient, in the absence of close and personal communication with the physician, sees the diagnostic test and results as the most important element of their care. It follows, doctors who do not order the latest diagnostic tests are not up to date. It also follows that the more complex, new and expensive the test, the better the care must be. The more this process continues, the less quality communication occurs. Do you see a problem here?

Many doctors do still spend time talking with their patients. These are the types of doctors you will want on your side should you become ill. After all, a doctor who wishes to explore a patient as a whole person (not just their broken part) is more likely to treat you as a Priority Patient!

Scripted Conversations...

Not only are doctors programmed with certain expected behaviours, they also acquire a set of well-worn phrases along the way, that they often use to achieve desired responses from their patients. Some phrases doctors might routinely use are:

Supportive Comments
-You can live a very long time with this problem.
-You look great! This treatment must agree with you!
-There is no evidence of deterioration.

Comments Designed to Maximize the Effect of the Treatment
-This will definitely make you feel better.
-These pills will do the job!
-Let's decrease the dose of your medication.

Comments Designed to Shock
-If you don't do this you will be dead in three months!
-If you can't follow my advice, don't bother coming back!
-If you continue to smoke you are killing yourself!
-I get paid to do this operation whether you listen to my advice or not!

Comments to Avoid Discussion
-Just do it.
-You don't need the details right now.
-You don't have the training to understand.

-I know he does not communicate well, but he is an excellent
  specialist, just do what he says!
-You don't need the test results, just let me handle that.
-You're not a doctor.

Comments to Build Trust

-Trust me, I'm a doctor!
-It's my speciality.
-It's just as simple as changing a part in your car.
-Trust me, I'll do my best for you (unfortunately you have no idea
  what his best is!!!!)

This is not to imply that what your doctor is saying is not genuine, in fact
he may not even realize that he has said it to hundreds of patients before
you. It simply means that these are phrases that they have been taught to
use in order to achieve a desired effect in their patient. The more your
doctor/patient relationship matures, the less of this programmed
commentary will occur. In the mean time, if you are aware of these phrases,
you will know where you doctor is coming from, and why he is saying it.
You will develop an understanding of what he is trying to achieve.

The Many Types Of Office Practice

There are many different types of office practice for doctors. The original
model for a doctor's office was a single practitioner caring for a group of
patients. He was always available to them, day and night and even made
house calls. Those days are gone. Today, doctors may enter into many
other types of office practice. All of these have a variable effect on interactions
with patients.

Solo Practice

The solo practice is decreasing in popularity for family physicians, but it
remains standard for specialists. The family doctor is now more likely to
share office space with at least one other physician. Expenses are shared
and patients are not without help when one doctor is away. Two or more
solo practitioners may even cover each other for meetings and holidays.
This is an unattractive model for new young physicians interested in lifestyle.

Group Practice

Some doctors group together not only to share expenses, but to share
patients as well. Sometimes this is in the same office, sometimes in the
same building. There are many variations. In some situations, the group

model will ensure that you see 'your' doctor each visit, while others will have you seen by 'a' doctor each visit. In other words, the patients may be 'pooled' into one large practice. This model is encouraged by various primary care reform advocates. Watch for changes to come.

Walk-In Clinics

Walk-in clinics are organized in such a way that any patient can 'show up' or 'drop in' during business hours which generally extend into the evening, and the doctor(s) on call will see them. Generally patients do not see their doctor, but *any available* doctor. This type of medical practice delivers care on a 'problem basis' not a 'personal basis'. If you don't have a personal physician this will solve your problem temporarily. Don't expect them to communicate with your personal physician. There is lots of variation in this model as well; your personal physician may work in a walk-in clinic at night. While these clinics can be very useful for simple and quick fixes, they are not personalized enough for continuous, in depth care. If the patient's condition is chronic requiring monitoring over a period of time, or severe such as in the case of an emergency, the patient will usually be referred elsewhere.

Health Maintenance Organization

These are relatively large organizations with management structures that employ physicians, nurses, secretaries and lab staff. These people are paid a salary for carrying out specific job descriptions. They have benefit programs including vacation and conference leave. You may or may not have your own personal physician in this model. If you attend the various physicians and specialists within this model your records are all in one place.

Emergency Department Practice

Many hospital emergency rooms are staffed by specially trained emergency physicians. These doctors may be salaried by the hospital or self-employed. They work shifts of 8-12 hours. Their job is to care for patients who come to the hospital emergency room for medical care. Historically family doctors performed this function. With the increasing demand for specialized training, emergency medical specialists have filed this role. They are specifically trained to handle multiple serious physical injuries as well as crisis situations. There is rarely any follow-up or attention paid to chronic conditions. It should be appreciated that most medical interactions are not emergencies.

Industrial Medicine

Some physicians choose to work as full-time salaried employees of large business organizations, with many employees.

Doctors Are People Too!

Although many things shape a doctor's behaviour and beliefs, he is also influenced daily by a wide range of other forces that may or may not be directly related to practising medicine. Like everyone else, doctors play a number of roles in life, each with its unique responsibilities. You can see how your physician may be preoccupied with other issues.

Doctors Have Many Roles

- Business people – They have all of the concerns of operating an office.
- Parents – They worry about their children like everyone else.
- Children – They may have elderly parents to care for.
- Tenants – They are subject to all of the problems of renting office space.
- Landlords – They may have to cope with tenants.
- Employers – They must hire and manage staff.
- Employees – They often have all of the concerns that accompany any job.
- Clients – They must deal with patients.
- Investors – They can lose or make money just like anyone else.
- Inventors – They are sometimes occupied by creative enterprises.
- Voters – They too, follow politics.
- Politicians – They are often leaders in the community.
- Committee members – They may work on various committees.
- Members of boards – They may serve on hospital boards.
- Community fund-raisers – They may be involved in charitable organizations.
- Mentors – They often have students who wish to learn from them.
- Educators – Some even teach at universities and in medical schools.
- Students – They are obliged to stay current.
- Researchers – Some pursue new knowledge.
- Etc., etc., etc.

Now that you have gained some insight into what goes into becoming a doctor, maintaining a practice, and managing a physician's way of life, it is easy to see (with all of these responsibilities) why some days your doctor may not approach your problem in the manner in which you had hoped. It is up to the patient in these situations, to understand and to recognize when the doctor is distracted, but at the same time to insist on the doctor's undivided attention. If it is not possible, book another appointment and hope for a better result the next time! If the doctor is *always* too distracted and your attempts to get the attention you need go unrecognized, it is time to search for someone who hopefully will treat you like a Priority Patient!

Keys To The Doctor's Office

When it becomes necessary to take your problem to your personal physician, always be prepared in advance in order to get the most from your visit. All too often people come away from a doctor's appointment with unanswered questions, confusion and sometimes, even fear. Much of that is because they were unprepared. If prepared for your visit, you will ask the right questions and at the same time, give your doctor enough information to help choose an appropriate treatment strategy. You will also be prepared to listen and record. Most important, realize that you must connect with your physician. Make sure that you are both on the same page and that he clearly understands your complaint in detail. If he knows you well, he will understand *why* you want to choose certain options.

Before You Go - Be In The Know

It is important to know exactly why you are going to see your doctor. Arriving and telling him that you "just don't feel well" is not enough. Always bring a list of concerns for your doctor. It is of pivotal importance that you describe your symptom or complaint as clearly and completely as possible. Try to recall all of the details of your complaint, including: the time it started, what you were doing, how long it persisted, how severe it was, how it affected you, what if anything you did. Sometimes people know what triggered their complaint but neglect to mention it. Lots of information is forgotten or felt to be unimportant. The doctor's interpretation of the cause of your symptom relies entirely on the patient's description. This is why the doctor asks so many questions; it's the answers that guide him to the solution.

The description of your symptom is extremely important and you are the only one who can describe it!

What To Bring....Lists, Lists & More Lists

Always be sure to write everything down. We all think we know what we want to say (or ask), until we are in the office environment and feel flustered and rushed. It is far too easy at that point to forget the important things you wanted to remember. It's always a good idea to have someone you trust accompany you. Remembering what the doctor said isn't easy. Your accompanying friend or relative may also help you understand and make decisions if necessary.

What To Bring

- List of questions you want to ask
- Family member or friend to help you remember
- List of your current medications and their doses
- The actual pill bottles
- Description of reactions to either past or present medications
- List of drug allergies
- List of alternative or home remedies you are taking
- List of prescriptions you need renewed
- Your personal health diary (any records you have kept regarding your health care)
- Change for parking meters, a recent magazine, etc.

For the doctor's benefit as well as your own, you should always bring your list of current medications and doses. You will also want to bring your personal health care diary (records you have kept regarding your health). It is often preferred that you bring the actual pill bottles so that there are no mistakes as to what you are taking. Don't hesitate to tell your doctor if you are taking any alternative or home remedies. Some alternative or herbal treatments may interact with your prescription drugs and this information is crucial to ensure your safety as well as the effectiveness of your treatment plan.

While you are preparing for your visit to the doctor's office, it is a good idea to consider which prescriptions you will need to have renewed. Don't hesitate to ask for several repeats if you will be on the medication for a long time. This could save both you and your doctor unnecessary visits. Remember, the quality of the visit to your doctor's office can be enhanced by YOU; you get out what you put in.

Talking With The Doctor

There is one thing patients should remember during the visit to the doctor's office: be polite, firm and to the point. Never allow yourself to feel rushed. You need clear answers to your questions and clear instructions on how to continue to manage your health life. Your doctor's time (as well as your own) is wasted if you go home and do not know what you are supposed to do or why. We list a few useful questions on the following page.

★ ★ ★ ★ ★

"Be engaged and involved in the care [you are] getting"

Dr. Harlan Krumholz
A.C.C. Practice News · January, 2003

ASK

- Is this more of a nuisance problem or is it serious/life threatening?
- How did I catch this illness or what caused this to happen?
- Is it contagious?
- Should I be concerned about my children?
- Do I need to take time off work or restrict certain activities?
- Can this be cured completely?
- How long will it take to recover?
- What are my treatment options?
- How effective is the treatment?

If you do not understand what your doctor said, keep asking questions until you feel you understand. Remember, the doctor may appear to give superficial answers. This may be because he is too busy. He may feel you could not possibly comprehend a detailed medical description. The opposite may also be true. Your doctor may lose you in unnecessary detailed medical jargon. However, as the interview unwinds it is very important to understand clearly what is happening and why.

You're Still Confused

- Request a better explanation.
- Write it down.
- If possible ask him to draw you a picture.
- If there are statistics involved please record them.
- Request written material or a website address for further information.
- Ask for an early follow-up appointment (go through it again if necessary).

Diagnostic Options - Yes You Do Have Options!

Should your personal physician recommend that you go for diagnostic testing (tests designed to help him make an accurate diagnosis) you should ask what he hopes to learn from the results. You may want to ask the following:

ASK MORE

- Can this test hurt me?
- Will a sedative or anaesthetic be required?
- How is the test performed?
- Are there any injections involved?
- Is this test accurate or can there be
  false positives and false negatives?
- How might the test results affect my treatment?
- Does the laboratory have good quality control procedures
  and are they equipped to handle problems should they occur?

Treatment Options - Your Health, Your Choice

Once the doctor knows the cause of your problem (the diagnosis), you may be presented with a few treatment options. Prepare to ask for an explanation of each available option. Your doctor may choose the alternative he feels most appropriate for you. You need to know why he has chosen a particular option. Ask if you can speak to a patient who has also chosen this option. You may indicate a preference for one of the others. You are now demonstrating active participation in your health care. If your options are limited or represent risk, you certainly can request a second opinion. You are not insulting your doctor. Ask how each choice will affect the following:

- Returning to work
- Exercise
- Emotional stress
- Your Diet
- Your sex life
- Length of life
- Quality of life

Ask other important questions regarding your treatment options such as:

KEEP ASKING

- Will I be cured by this treatment, or is it simply
  going to relieve my symptoms?
- How successful is this particular treatment?
- How long does this treatment take?
- How will I know if it is working?
- What are the risks attached to this procedure?
- Can I take more than one of the treatment options?
- In what order should I take them?
- What are the chances that I could be worse?

Prescriptions - A Little Knowledge Can Save You!

Should your doctor give you a prescription, here are some important things to ask to make certain that you understand and can follow your doctor's instructions:

Understanding Your Prescription

- Why am I receiving it? – Get the specific reason or rationale for the particular drug.
- How will the drug affect me? – What should change, what should you watch out for?
- What are the serious side effects? - What should stop you from continuing the drug.
- Will the side effects stop when the medication is stopped?
- Find out how long you will be taking it.
- Is there information that you may read about this medication?

Long-term medications

If you are going to take this medication for months or years, request a 2 month prescription with 3 to 6 repeats. This will save both you and your doctor time, money and effort. Not all prescription renewals require an appointment. Imagine the time saved going to the pharmacy and the money saved on parking and dispensing fees.

Doctor/Patient Follow-up - Build A Lasting Relationship

There are several ways to ensure proper follow-up of your condition while minimizing unnecessary repeat visits and testing. Always request a copy of the test results. Keep them in your health diary for future reference. This may help you avoid unnecessary repeat testing and may assist other physicians in the future. If you are referred to a specialist try to obtain a copy of his consultation note for your records. It is important to get this as soon as you can, as it may be difficult to obtain later. Create a correspondence section in your health diary devoted to this type of information.

Whenever you are tested, record the name of the test, date, location and test result if available. Don't be surprised if the results of the diagnostic test are confusing to you personally. The copy is for you, the interpretation takes training. Have the results explained in detail, since they may significantly affect your treatment. Recognise that the results of these tests and how they change over time can affect your treatment.

Lastly, it is important to discuss the test results with your personal physician. You should never assume that no news is good news. Always find out the result of *every* test! Priority Patients always record these results. If the test results indicate that the treatment path is correct then proceed. If not, discuss further options.

Chapter Summary

☛   **Be Prepared.**

☛   **Know and describe your symptoms clearly.**

☛   **Bring your health care diary to every visit.**

☛   **Record as much as you can.**

☛   **Be polite, firm and to the point.**

☛   **Understand what is happening to you.**

☛   **Know your options.**

☛   **Connect with your doctor.**

Secrets Of The Referral Process

Being sent to a specialist may seem simple enough, but indeed it can be a very complex process. You might think that your personal physician is referring you to a particular specialist because he has the expertise required or because he is the best person to match your personality. Either could be the case...or neither. Regardless of his reasoning, it is vital that you ensure that both physicians communicate not only with you but with one another as well.

★ ★ ★ ★ ★

"Doctors cannot provide good diagnosis and treatment without full information"

George Radwanski
The Medical Post · November, 2002

Traditional Referral

Some personal physicians always refer patients to the same doctor in a particular speciality. This is probably because they have built a relationship over the years such that there is an understanding regarding each other's expectations. For example, the *referring physician* always supplies the specialist's office with sufficient historical notes, lab test results, description of the problem, and a reason for the referral. The *specialist* is known to fully assess the patient, he clearly communicates issues, gives directions, and subsequently corresponds with the referring doctor covering the issues and suggested plan of action.

It is also possible that the referring physician sends patients to a particular specialist because he knows exactly what that specialist will do and that is what he wants done. Otherwise, he might refer elsewhere; in other words, the personal physician does not want an opinion from the specialist, he simply wants a particular action. Maybe the referring physician and the particular specialist have other relationships: golf, education, business, geographic location, etc.

Conventional Referral

It is very different today! While the traditional referral mechanism is still active, it is much less active than before. New varieties of professional practice have created new referral patterns. There are many other reasons today for a referring physician to choose a certain specialist. Some of these reasons might include:

Conventional Reasons For Referral

- Type of Practice (special expertise, research interest)
- Location of practice
- Hospital affiliation (access to hospital resources)
- Availability
- On call (after hours)
- Language or culture
- Personal relationship (business, friends, family)
- Perceived match to the patient's personality
- Physician bias

Unfortunately, in some ways, the patient is increasingly sent to whichever specialist is available or on call for receiving new patients. If the referral is for a hospitalized patient, it will go to the specialist designated as on call for referral that day. None of the other important reasons for referral will apply. If the referral is for an office patient, it could be made for any of the other reasons, but *availability* will dominate over most other circumstances. To a large extent, this implies that anyone will do or a 'doc is a doc'. This type of practice and reasoning is more common now that health care personnel are in short supply. There is very little competition. Fragmentation of care seems more and more acceptable to both doctors and patients probably because few recognise the implications.

Why Is The Referral Taking So Long?

There are reasons why the referral to a specialist may take a long time. Here are a few reasons why your appointment may be delayed:

Reasons Your Appointment Is Delayed

- Request was not sent.
- Request was not received
- Inadequate information was sent.
- Office inefficiency
- Office processing time
- Perceived not urgent
- Speciality type (all such doctors are busy)
- Busy or popular practice selected

In most cases you won't have to do anything but wait. However if the referral seems to be taking a long time, it is always a good idea to phone both your doctor's office and the office of the specialist to 1) ensure that the request was received and 2) an appointment will be made, and 3) you will be notified by a specific date.

Who Gets In First?

Specialists have a variety of methods for coping with the number of patients that are referred to them. They vary significantly, but usually have a strategy for placing patients in order. Some patients are moved to the 'head of the pack' for many reasons, only one of which is perceived urgency. Perhaps some are already Priority Patients!

Ways of Deciding When Patients Are Seen

- Severity of illness
- Next in line
- 1st come, 1st served
- Interesting cases seen early
- Time standards (certain diagnosis must been seen within a certain time frame, e.g. cancer)
- Delayed necessary diagnostic testing
- Direct (verbal) request seen more quickly

How Can Your Doctor Get You In?

There are some instances where your doctor may want to speed up the referral process. In these situations, your doctor may do some or all of the following to help the process. If you can be of assistance, by all means do so.

How Referring Physicians Can Speed Up Referrals

- Write as well as call the specialist's office.
- Send a legible and complete referral request.
- Prepare the patient for the initial interview.
- Make the case sound interesting.
- Identify the patient as a Priority Patient
- Let the office know that a family member will be attending.
- Emphasize that the patient is cooperative.
- Be very specific about the question being asked.
- Call in a favour.

With a little luck, your doctor will be able to get the specialist to see you as soon as possible. The important thing is that you communicate with your doctor. Be clear about your concerns regarding the time it takes to be seen by a specialist, and always ask questions. Find out if your doctor can refer you to someone else sooner and ask his opinion on the particular specialist. You will want to read the following chapter on preparing for a visit to the specialist.

Chapter Summary

- Find out how serious your condition is.

- Ask your doctor how long it is safe to wait to see the specialist.

- Ask if there are alternatives (treatments, specialists, etc.)

- Track your health while you wait to be seen.

- Report any changes in your condition right away.

- All doctors appreciate your efforts to save their time!

- Request a specialist with a personality similar to yours.

Keys To The Specialist

Preparing for a visit with a specialist can be quite a different experience compared to the average visit with your personal physician. If your doctor is sending you to a specialist for a consultation, there are procedures you should follow to ensure that you get the most out of the visit. You do not want to waste your time or the specialist's, but you do want to be certain that you are getting the full benefit of the consulting doctor's expertise. Your doctor is sending you to a specialist to obtain his expert opinion about a specific aspect of your illness. For example a cardiologist will be asked to assess for the presence and severity of heart disease. Each time you are referred to a specialist it should be clear *why* you are going and *what* you should expect. This chapter is written to help you actively participate in the process of obtaining expert opinion regarding your care. Do not underestimate this opportunity.

The Referral

If you are referred to a specialist, record the specialist's name, office number, address and reason for referral. You probably think this should be a very easy process. It isn't! It can be very complicated. It is fraught with all kinds of problems including missed or cancelled appointments. It is quite possible that a planned appointment was never even arranged. Do not be afraid to call if you have not been given your appointment date and time. If your appointment is cancelled, make sure it is re-booked and ask that it not be cancelled a second time. Get the appointment date and *write it down*! Don't forget! Both doctors and patients put in a lot of time and effort to arrange these visits. Given the opportunity you might state your preferences with regard to the specialist's sex, office location and access. It would be wise to obtain the following information from your personal physician before you go:

Going To The Specialist - Things You Need To Know

- When will the specialist become aware of the referral?
- Is the request being faxed, phoned or mailed?
- Be aware of the average waiting period for this referral.
- Will you have to wait days, weeks or months?
- Is this waiting time acceptable for your condition?
- If the waiting time is *not* acceptable (to you or your doctor) ask that something be done to shorten it.
- If the referral is out of town, ask for travel and accommodation information.
- Ask both offices if you are required to make personal preparations for the visit or bring special items.

It wouldn't hurt to phone the specialist's office in advance and ask if there is anything you should bring or be aware of prior to the appointment. Assume that your specialist knows your name and not much else. Realize that it is common practice for physicians to not communicate details prior to a consultation. If you have a personal health care diary, offer to supply the specialist's secretary a copy in advance. This will save her time both before and on the day of your appointment.

Priority Patients will assist by taking any referral information with them to the specialist. This will ensure information is not misplaced or forgotten. In the case of x-rays try to pick them up and bring them with you rather than relying on a courier or other means of transfer. They must be returned. You don't want your appointment affected by missing information or test results. Always do your best to ensure that the specialist has received all necessary information. By doing so, you will more than likely negate the need for an unnecessary follow-up visit. Maximize! Remember, you are only one of thousands of patients referred to specialists every day. The only person to ensure that it is done right is YOU!

What To Bring With You

You must bring as much of your patient history and test results with you as possible. In this situation, a personal health diary is indispensable. The specialist does not know you. He is starting from scratch! Assume they have incomplete information regarding your problem. Always try to bring a family member or close friend with you. Bring your prescriptions with you (the original containers are best). Be prepared to list any alternative or herbal remedies that you may be taking. Do not forget to bring all of your relevant insurance information, along with your health card. Your doctor's office may *not* forward this information with the referral. For example, don't forget:

- A complete description of your symptoms
- A summary of your complaint in detail
- A list of questions
- Your general treatment preferences

During The Appointment

Understand, details of your personal health history are unknown to the specialist. They will focus on your current complaint. Decisions regarding diagnostic testing and treatment options are best customized to you as an individual and should take into account your preferences and choices. You will need to communicate these preferences to the specialist very clearly! Your specialist will need to understand what is important for you as an individual. Remember you have not yet established a rapport with this specialist. He must know who you are. Every patient has different needs. When faced with the same illness and treatment options, they choose differently. For example, an eighty-year-old patient may not want to risk triple bypass surgery whereas a forty-year-old would take the opportunity gladly! Together with your specialist, you will weigh your needs against the possible outcomes of any testing or procedures (referred to as risk vs. benefit). Never allow something to be done simply because it is the fashionable therapy of the day. Do not assume that the specialist can choose what is best for you until he knows you well enough. Some general questions that you may want to ask your specialist are:

Example Questions For Your Specialist

- May I call your office for a follow-up appointment?
- How long will I have to wait for an appointment?
- Will you refill prescriptions outside your specialty?
- What are the possible treatment *options*?
- What are the possible outcomes of each option?
- Are there videos that I may view to help me prepare for tests, etc.?
- Is one surgical centre preferable over the others?

There are many potential outcomes from this consultation. You may be quite satisfied, you may be very upset. If you are uncomfortable with the specialist and the direction he is taking (e.g. you are only given one option), do not be afraid to ask for a second opinion. Many consumers will consult with several salespeople before buying a new car or get several estimates on repairs for a project at home. Why feel forced to accept only one opinion when it comes to something as serious as your health? When the interview is completed and you have been given specialist advice you should take some time to consider what you have been told and what your options are. Some will do that immediately; others will take much longer. You should discuss the interview with your personal physician. Misunderstandings might be clarified by a brief follow-up appointment with the specialist. If a second opinion is necessary, it can be arranged. However, remember ultimately you make the final decision about your care. Specialists will not always agree, but they should supply you with all of the options that are available and the risks and benefits of each.

Frequently people allow important decisions to be made for them particularly when they are feeling vulnerable in the midst of a medical problem. At these times their choices may be different than they would be if they were feeling healthy and confident. No patient should be a passive observer. Even if the system seems to view you as just another patient, you're not. But it's up to you to demonstrate your individuality.

Follow-Up

Your follow-up plan may include a return visit to your specialist or an appointment with your personal physician. Many specialists do not see patients in follow-up unless it is requested. It will likely depend on your particular medical problem. If the specialist did not find something within his expertise that he could help you with, your problem may be clarified by referral to a specialist in another field. Otherwise, having ruled out the suspected and perhaps feared diagnosis, your doctor should adopt other treatment strategies.

As with all testing and treatments, you should always follow-up with a phone call or appointment to ensure that the results have been read and interpreted (not merely filed and forgotten). Request a copy of all test results and be sure that a copy is received by your doctor's office. Although it may be difficult (as specialists are often quite busy), ask the specialist for your treatment plan in writing.

Chapter Summary

- Ask your doctor to 'match' the specialist to *you* not just *your problem.*

- Assume the specialist knows nothing about you.

- Ensure you are referred as a *patient with a problem*, not just a *problem!*

- Bring everything in your arsenal (files, prescription bottles, test results, etc.).

- Don't be put on eternal waiting lists with multiple cancellations!

- Maximize your time with the specialist!

- Make sure you clearly understand the diagnosis and treatment *before* leaving the office!

- Make every effort to have the specialist deal with you directly (not just with your family doctor).

Introduction To Hospitals And You: Welcome Stranger!

You firmly believe that the health care system and the medical establishment are taking care of *you*. You firmly believe that all the components of the health care system communicate with each other and share information about *you*. You are convinced that your personal physician (if you have one) receives correspondence about you from hospitals, walk-in clinics, specialists, emergency rooms, etc. You believe that the specialist has all the necessary information about you before you go for the consultation. Not always so!

You have prepaid for your health care either through insurance premiums, income tax and payroll deductions. You have prepaid so you expect service when you need it. You assume the health care system is well organized, high tech, responsive, capable, modern, efficient, etc. You assume that because you have 'prepaid' they are 'prepared' to deal with you and your particular problem. Not always so!

You... Are A Stranger

You are a stranger. If you have a personal physician, his office is open 9 - 5 Monday to Friday perhaps with Wednesday afternoon off. This is 40 hours per week or less. A 7-day week consists of (7 X 24 hours) 168 hours. That means your personal physician is only available to you 40 out of 168 hours. That is the equivalent of less than 25% of the time! In many cases it is less. If you get sick and call your personal physician, there is a good chance you will be told to go to the hospital emergency room or wait days for an appointment. If your call is not answered, you may find yourself in a walk-in clinic.

Now, you are definitely a stranger. If you only have a cold, it may not matter unless you are prescribed an antibiotic to which you are allergic. If you have a complex medical problem (diabetes, heart disease, recent surgery) it does matter. You do not remember and you have no available record. The doctor you are about to see in the clinic or the emergency room has no historical knowledge of you or your condition. If it is after hours or on weekends, that information is not readily available.

You are a stranger to 99% of the health care system. Information about you is more or less available during the regular working hours (less than 25% of the week, God help you over Christmas and New Year's)! That means, 75% of the time you are going to be taken care of by a stranger who has never met you before and has no knowledge of your medical conditions, your philosophy of life, your attitudes regarding medical care or your desire not to be treated under certain circumstances, etc. He has no knowledge of you, of your allergies, your blood group or your previous encounters with the medical establishment. Do not be surprised if the questions you are asked in this encounter have been asked of you many, many times before. That's the system!

You are indeed a stranger! And guess what! You are interacting with the medical establishment (the system) in the busiest, most impersonal, loudest, most inappropriate, most hectic, least communicative environment possible! This is the ultimate in 'piece work', fragmentation of care at its best! Focus is on the problem, not on the patient. In the emergency room, if you are not apparently going to die within the next 24 hours, why are you here? Welcome stranger!

Fragmentation In Health Care

If you are happy with fragmented health care, carry on. If not, I suggest you listen. For the foreseeable future, you will be exposed to more health professionals who simply don't know you. They will have very limited information about you in *their* file, if they have one. They will most certainly not have *all* the relative information that should be available to them even if it does exist somewhere else. It will be difficult for them to obtain even with your specific and expressed consent. Please, do not assume that health care professionals communicate well with one another regarding your health!

★ ★ ★ ★ ★

"There is no health-care system. Or, more precisely, no single system; but rather, a confusing collection of wholly separate systems, each scrambling valiantly to serve its own notions of what is good for you, often at cross-purposes with the next, often unable to get the most basic information from one stage to the next"

Toronto Star Staff in a week-long report titled: Code Zero

Toronto Star • May, 2002

So What Can You Do?

For now, the best thing patients can do is be knowledgeable about the system, be prepared for your encounters with health care professionals and keep excellent records of your health information. Ask as many questions as necessary to understand what is being done. Above all else, when dealing with those who do not know you, *identify yourself!* Never (not even when you see your specialist in the hospital hallway) assume that they know you for even a minute. Remember; you are a stranger!

Review the highlights of this introduction.

1) **Identify yourself.**

2) **Identify yourself again.**

3) **Identify yourself yet again.**

4) **Lead or be led by the health care professionals.**

5) **Assume they know very little about you.**

6) **Settle for their incomplete records or maintain your own complete health care file.**

7) **Even if you have a personal physician, they are not available to you 75% of the time!**

8) **Institutions exist to perform important 'piece work'.**

"The waiting list for cardiac bypass surgery...here has grown so long that not even an army of doctors working around the clock could restore the hospital's safe-wait guidelines"

Ann Graham Walker
The Medical Post · August, 2001

"Widespread fiddling and interference with the waiting lists may have 'prolonged the suffering' of patients or even worsened their condition"

Karen Birchard
The Medical Post · October, 2002

"As many as one in every eight Canadians apparently has unmet health-care needs, according to a Statistics Canada survey"

Ken Pole
The Medical Post · March, 2002

It's No Secret - You're Waiting
Welcome To C-AIR CANADA

When you seek medical attention, you are put through a process called *triage*. Triage is the term that refers to how patients are prioritized. It is why a person who has come to the ER after you might be seen before you. You and your complaint are rank ordered according to a perceived degree of urgency. It is a necessary process in the management of large numbers of patients. You will find formal triage procedures in hospital emergency rooms and on certain waiting lists such as heart surgery.

There are also informal triage processes in your doctor's or specialist's office and testing laboratories. Triage in these circumstances, is usually performed by a secretary or nurse. Many good doctors' offices are careful to ask why a patient needs a particular appointment and how severe is their problem. They make an effort to sort their patients according to perceived medical need, sicker patients first. Other offices operated on a first come first served basis. Can you tell the difference?

Many patients don't understand why they must give details about their complaint when making an appointment. Who is at fault if they minimize their complaint on the phone? It is important that you understand how triage works in order to ensure your proper place in line. Do you see why you need to be clear and concise!

You're Late, You're Late, For A Very Important Date

Yes, we are waiting. Sometimes we are waiting hours in the emergency room at 2:00 am surrounded by strangers and health care workers we have never seen before and will never see again! More frequently, we are waiting days or weeks for an appointment with the family physician or specialist, a diagnostic test, a test result, a visiting nurse or a date for hospitalization. There seems no end to the line-ups. We may be in several before finding the solution to a single problem! Health care is one of the very few businesses in which the customer is always kept waiting.

What most people don't realize is the combined amount of total time a patient can be kept waiting. And guess what; most of the time you are invisible. And guess what; you can be forgotten! At a time when society is spending even more money on increasingly sophisticated computer-based communications and information-gathering systems, patients are waiting longer and longer. It's quite bizarre because you are (or a least should be) the most important element of the health care universe.

As patients, we want to believe that our comfort and well being are the primary goals of the medical establishment. All those professionals exist to help us in our 'time of need'. But do they really? We feel that we are the centre of their attention and they are dedicated to helping us. Their focus is on us. Or is it? Unfortunately, access to the Canadian health care system is neither simple nor easy. Rapidity and convenience are not words commonly associated with this system. We are allowed access in a time frame convenient to the system.

The system as we know it functions as such because we tolerate and accept the current conditions. It is believed to be fair. Unlike emergency departments in hospitals that have developed methods for patient sorting (triage), most line-ups are not well sorted and are even random in nature. In the emergency department every effort is made to treat the sickest patient first. The walk-in clinic likely functions on the basis of first come first served. The personal physician's office usually has no formal mechanism for sorting patients. The secretary serves as the 'booking agent' and decides how you will be prioritized and when you will be seen. Your place in line may be one of the most important aspects of your care. You assume it was determined in a fair and just fashion. You probably thought that your waiting time was always based on the severity of your illness.

What Do Airports And Airplanes Have To Do With Anything?

If you think about the Canadian health care system as a series of airplanes (patients) and airports (health services), these concepts will be easier to understand. Airports are expensive, few in number, and may be large or small. They may also be overcrowded, subject to busy periods, or temporary closure. They are not unlike hospitals.

Large urban emergency rooms when stretched frequently divert ambulance patients to other hospitals. When airports are busy and their landing strips are full, they delay the landing of incoming flights. Airports are congested by weather, runways out of service, labour unrest, accidents, inadequate equipment or sheer volume. When these conditions occur, the airport will stack up airplanes and put them into a holding pattern. Although these practices are designed to maintain safety and efficiency, other safety issues arise due to the delays! The same is true of patients waiting. Does the emergency department waiting room remind you of an airport lounge when flights are cancelled?

Patients are also placed in sequence (holding pattern) in emergency rooms, doctors' appointment books and walk-in clinics. Not all airplanes are the same. Some cannot stay in holding pattern indefinitely due to limited fuel. The situation could get serious if they were forced to wait too long. Not all patients waiting are the same. Some should not wait for desperately needed services. Some can wait.

Airplanes have the benefit of a pilot and crew who can intervene in the delaying process when it is obvious that a particular aircraft must land. Similarly, not all patient line-ups have the benefit of an observant pilot and crew. In fact most don't. Unlike airplanes, patients don't necessarily know how significant their medical problem is until assessed. Frequently it is the assessment that is delayed. The only obvious warning gauge for the patient is how sick you feel. You are the pilot. It is primarily up to you to notify others of any change in your status.

Canadian hospitals do not quickly adjust availability of their services based on patient demand. Doctor's offices do not expand or increase the volume of patients they can handle simply because there are more patients needing services. Instead, the system stacks up its patients putting them into a holding pattern; a delaying tactic that allows the hospital (clinic or office) to maintain a budgeted level of throughput. This throughput is more likely based on quantity rather than quality. Business as usual! The number of patients waiting, the size of the list, will vary from time to time.

C-AIR Traffic Control And Security

Airports have rules and procedures to handle air traffic control, passenger service, baggage handling and communication. In the health care establishment, patients encounter institutional rules and treatment guidelines established to maintain efficiency and control of patient flow, bed (resource) utilization, medical record maintenance and data management. Unfortunately, we have all seen what happens when rules are rigid and do not allow for special circumstances. Everyone knows someone who has either lost their luggage at the airport or lost their dentures in the hospital. Ever tried to get a copy of a hospital file? How much did it cost? Some rules may seem excessive; the price of confidentiality?

Airplanes are mechanical and electrical in nature with component parts that have performance ratings that are under warranty because they are predictable. Patients are not predictable! Diseases affecting human physiology can be abrupt in onset, instantaneously critical in nature and occur without warning. Although we use words like 'stable' or 'unstable' when describing a patient's current status, we are in fact describing the past, not predicting the future. Yesterday's 'stable' patient is now 'unstable'. Patients do not come with warning lights!

Thank You For Flying 'Canada Health C-AIR'

There is little one can do when they encounter an inflexible barrier to health care. However there are a few things you can do to help you understand and possibly better endure the waiting process. After all, Canadian health care will not change over night – The section "The Key to Surviving the Waiting Game" will give you tools that will help you to speed up the process, or at least better endure the typical waiting period. So buckle up, secure your tray and make sure your seat is in the upright position.

Keys To The Emergency Department

What patients need to understand is that the emergency department was meant to care for *emergencies*. However, it is now often used as a convenience for 'drive-thru' medical service. It is regarded by many as a 'clinic' when they may take *all* complaints. If it is not convenient to wait for their family doctor, people simply go to the emergency room! Why are we doing this? Frequently there appear to be no alternatives. Emergency room care is fragmented, impersonal and often a band-aid solution to your current problem. There was a time when 'continuity of care' was felt to be the best strategy in caring for patients. The emergency room deals with the problem of the moment, not the before or the after, but the now! You will be looked after by strangers who know nothing about your health problems and who have little time to pursue issues in depth.

Going To The ER

It is wise to know how your local emergency department functions in advance of needing its services. In many instances, a visit to the emergency room (ER) *is* necessary. It is not the purpose of this book to tell you *when* or *when not* to go to the ER. You will make that decision based on your need at the time. Please, respect the fact that the emergency room is for *true* emergencies! Today however, people visit the emergency room for many reasons other than true medical emergencies.

Examples of non-emergency visits	**True emergency visits**
-prescription renewals	-severe bleeding
-routine annual examinations	-loss of consciousness
-common cold	-persistent vomiting
-familiar complaints	-motor vehicle accident
-doctors office closed	-obvious fracture
-no family doctor	-head injury
-trying to fast-track health care	-chest pain with known heart disease

When emergency rooms reach their capacity, they frequently go on redirect (in large cities), which means that patients cannot be accommodated and are redirected to the next closest hospital ER department. In smaller towns, with one hospital there is no choice.

What To Bring

Once you've decided to go, be prepared to wait unless you are the highest priority! It is always wise to bring a few necessary items to the emergency room, as even the simplest complaint can turn into an overnight stay. Here is a list of emergency room essentials:

ER Essentials

- Always bring money in the form of coins for parking, vending machines and phone calls (don't forget transportation home).
- Write out your symptoms in detail and bring it for the doctor.
- All of your medications (bottles preferably), so the doctor will know exactly what you are taking
- Your personal health care diary and all of your available medical history
- Your doctor's name and phone number (include your specialist's as well)
- A list of your allergies – this is very important, as the ER may not have any records on you

Bringing The Young Or Elderly To The ER

If you are bringing a child or an elderly person bring:

- An activity such as a book or crayons (it is a much longer wait when your child is sick *and* bored!)
- Any incontinence supplies that you will need for a 12-hour period (such as diapers, absorbent undergarments, catheters, a change of pants, etc.)
- Snacks – the best is usually crackers as they are easily digested even when ill (snacks *must* be cleared by the nurse or doctor).
- If necessary, bring a few baby bottles (ready to use) and other supplies.
- In the case of the elderly person, bring their personal phone book so that you may contact people for them.
- Their medical history and records as well as a list of contacts (doctors, specialists, etc.)
- In the case of the child, a favourite toy or teddy bear for comfort

A pre-packed emergency bag with the above items and more is always a good idea. Include a fair amount of change, as you will always need more than you bring.

First Stop - Ask For Assistance

When you arrive at the emergency room identify yourself and spell your last name. If you are registering for someone else, state your relationship to the patient. Clearly state your most serious complaint. Ask how long the approximate waiting period will be. Remember you will wait in the waiting room and then you may also wait in the examining room. If the wait is long, make yourself comfortable. Use this time to record the details of your complaint and update your health care diary. Ask if there are any restrictions on your moving about or eating and drinking. Find out how you will know when it is your turn. You may want to periodically make certain that you have not been forgotten. Do not be afraid to ask how much longer you can expect to wait (especially if you have been waiting for a long time).

The Triage Process

Understand that when you arrive, the emergency room does not work on a first-come, first-serve basis. It operates on the premise that the more severe and life-threatening problems are dealt with first. Most Canadian hospitals adhere to a standardized management scheme. This scheme allows the triage nurse to assess and rank order patients on their perceived degree of urgency. It is usually accomplished by following these basic rules:

1) Sick patients are seen first.
2) Triage is always done by an experienced nurse.
3) The patient is assigned a level of perceived severity (usually 1 to 5).
    e.g. Level 1 - major burns, cardiac arrest
        Level 2 – severe chest pain
        Level 3 – abdominal pain
        Level 4 – cut requiring stitches
        Level 5 - prescription renewal
4) The wait depends on your assigned level and how busy the department is (a level 1 person will always be seen immediately, no matter how busy the department).
5) A level 2 patient will be seen before a level 5.
6) If there are five level 3's they are seen in the order of arrival unless there is a change in their condition.

The Triage Nurse

Your first interview with health care personnel will be with the triage nurse. Your answers to her questions and their findings on examination will decide your level of urgency. It is unwise to knowingly mislead the triage nurse.

The information you give can be critical. Expect to be asked the following:

Minimum Information Required To Describe Symptoms

- Severity
- Duration and persistence
- Locations
- Onset
- What you were doing
- Last meal or drink
- New medications
- New activities
- Problems at home
- Allergies
- If it has happened before

You should never over or understate your problem. If you have severe pain do not say, "it hurts – but I'll live". Even if you are trying to lighten the situation, or trying not to appear weak or whiny, you could be giving the impression that your problem is not to be taken seriously. This will leave you sitting in the waiting room for hours. If for example you have severe pain in your abdomen, tell the admitting nurse that you have "constant and severe pain", not "a cramp in your tummy". Be very clear about where it hurts and how bad. Show the nurse and doctor the notes you made before your arrival.

When describing your problem, inform the nurse of any fluctuations in your condition. If you had a temperature, but once you arrived it had gone down, be sure to let them know how high your temperature was. Describe your reason for going to the emergency room with clear and descriptive words. If your condition worsens during the wait, don't be afraid to tell the nurse (she *must* be informed). Changes of any kind may indicate a need to reassess your condition, which may change your level of priority. This is a busy environment; you're one of the 'herd', and you are not being constantly monitored. Your level of urgency dictates the frequency of reassessments. Any illness that takes you to the ER can worsen quickly. You need to be polite but pro-active and firm. Do not *ever* verbally or physically attack any of the staff in the ER! You are in a vulnerable state, probably emotional and you may want to lash out, but such behaviour will *not* be rewarded nor tolerated! If appropriate, the police will be called and you can be charged.

The Emergency Department Physician

After you have been taken to a treatment room, the emergency physician will arrive to question and examine you. Begin with describing your symptoms. Again it is very important to explain your problem very clearly and in great detail. In the emergency room, most of the attention is given to the problem of the moment. All potentially relevant information (past or present) should be communicated to the physician. Having written this down in advance is a definite advantage! All of this is difficult for everyone in a hurried environment. Don't forget to tell the doctor vital information simply because you are being rushed.

Examples Of Vital Information To Give ER Doctors

- New medications you've been given
- Allergies that you may have
- What you were doing when it occurred
- Any new changes in you situation
- Any recent injuries or accidents
- If you have blood in urine or stools

Explain any contributing factors and relevant or related information that the doctor may need. Tell them if other family members are having similar problems. Recent travel information is important, as is recent hospitalization. This may also help the physician with his diagnosis.

Keep your health care diary with you and tell the doctor that you have it, in case he needs additional information. Tell the doctor about your allergies, any family history of illness, what prescriptions you are taking and any serious chronic ailments that you have. The physician will likely arrange for tests that will take some time to be completed. These could include blood tests, urine sample, x-rays, ECG, etc. Depending on your complaint and the results of these tests, you may be treated and discharged or admitted to hospital.

Plan For Going Home

If you are discharged, be sure to request that your personal physician be notified of your visit, and receive a copy of any notes or test results. Try to get a written copy of your diagnosis and treatment plan for your own records. If you are admitted, ask the nurse to notify your family and your doctor or specialist. You may want to phone and leave a message for your doctor to ensure that he knows where you are. Yes – you can ask for a phone!

Always write down the names of the physicians who are involved in your care while in the emergency room. Be sure to let them know that you want your personal physician involved in any major decisions that are to be made regarding your care. Discuss your treatment options with the emergency physician as you would with your own physician. If you have concerns or questions regarding the treatment, ask! Do not feel that because it is a fast-paced environment, your questions are unimportant. Remember, you are in a strange environment, being treated by strangers. They mean well but they don't know you. Fast-forward decision making is not necessarily wise!

The way you are treated in emergency departments will vary according to size, staffing, location, and number of similar facilities in the area.

Follow-Up

As with all appointments, make certain that you have a clear understanding of the problem and the treatment strategy. If you must wait for any additional testing, then use the time to record the summary of your visit including the date, time, and physician's name. If you are given any forms from the ER keep them in your file. There is a good chance that your physician will not receive information regarding your ER visit; you should make a point to inform them yourself. Always carry through with your treatment plan. If you are given antibiotics, take them until the prescription is completely finished, and always be sure to show up for any tests that the physician has requested. Lastly, ask if a follow-up visit with your own physician is necessary.

Chapter Summary

- **The ER is for Emergencies!**

- **ER care is isolated and specific to your current problem!**

- **Write everything down- especially names!**

- **Communication is limited outside the ER.**

- **You must inform your doctor about your trip to the ER.**

- **The ER does not usually do patient follow-up.**

Secrets About Hospitals

As patients we may appear to be boring and routine or rare and challenging 'cases' depending on our disease process and how fascinating we appear to the particular doctor involved. Similarly, to a hospital administrator, our medical problem may be straightforward and inexpensive or complex and very costly. We are certain that doctors, nurses, hospitals and others involved in the treatment of our illness are keeping track of our care, medications and progress, as part of the solution to the riddle of our disease. We want to believe that hospitals are completely safe environments. We hope to be accorded the same level of care regardless of the cost or fascination of our illness. We believe *quality control* and *accountability* are fundamental components of the health care system. Patients feel protected knowing that the Canada Health Act sets high standards, as do self-governing professional organizations. In summary, we have faith that the health care system's safety net will protect us from harm.

Unfortunately, laws against speeding do not stop people from driving too fast. We have all heard stories about professionals who for many years, behave unprofessionally before being identified and disciplined. Lately, we have been exposed to media reports demonstrating that medical errors in hospitals are much more common than we might have expected. Has this always been the case, or has something changed? Has quality control and level of patient safety been compromised in the name of efficiency? They now refer to us as 'clients', not 'patients'. Does that imply a more businesslike approach to medicine? Our hospitals can no longer escape the demands of fiscal responsibility. The business of medicine has always been big but never acted like big business. The quality of medical care you receive is now in competition with other corporate interests, even in Canada, eh?

If It's Not About The Patient, What Is It About?

Individual patients are extremely important, but are certainly not the only consideration for health care administrators. Today, health care professionals and hospital administrators constantly find themselves caught up in a difficult balancing act. What really does take priority? Much of a hospital's administrative activity represents development of necessary coping strategies which never seem to completely solve the problems. Society has witnessed a growing number of patients waiting in line for desperately needed operations because of shortages: doctors, nurses, beds, operating rooms. Strangely, entire wards of hospitals may be shut down, at times resembling ghost towns, closed in the name of efficiency. We are constantly told that these problems are due to inadequate funding.

Everyone will say that patients come first and have the highest priority. For example, a hospital may manage its budgeted 700 coronary bypass patients very well. However, was it the right 700 patients when in fact 850 were waiting? What about the other 150 patients in line? What criteria do the professionals and administrators use in the selection process? In the circumstance in which budget determines the number of patients treated, what happens to the *individual patient*? She is certainly not the centre of this universe. Is it possible that these institutional conditions influence physician and nurse action and behaviour? Today, it is definitely not your individual medical condition that determines priority. What indeed is the priority?

The Leaders And Their Priorities

There is no doubt, the various organizations in charge of health care delivery are working very hard to improve the system. Governments are looking for extra funding, improved efficiencies and ways of solving human resource issues. Medical societies and Associations are developing patient care plans and algorithms. Hospital management organizations (HMOs) look for improved efficiencies in health care delivery. Hospitals seek funding for new medical programs and expansion of existing ones!

These large organizations will help the system and the growing population of patients seeking even more complex and expensive medical care. Newer technologies allow more sophisticated care. Newer information systems will allow better preparation, budgeting, planning and execution of creative programs. But none of these large organizations put the individual patient first. None of them!

Service - The Non-Issue!

All of the new and great books on modern management concentrate solely on the leaders or members of a management team. They give examples like Hewlett Packard, IBM, Microsoft, and Xerox. They speak of their success being totally dependant on management style, with specific CEOs and company presidents taking the bulk of the credit. They mention the client or customer in passive terms suggesting that they naively follow some guru CEO's new philosophy or style with nothing better than a herd mentality. Funny, most of those big companies are now in trouble!

There have been few books (if any) written about hospital CEOs and their phenomenal successes. Despite the fact that Canadian medicine is a 100 billion dollar per year business, there are rarely any stock holder's meetings during which the investors (patients) can vote on the performance of companies (hospitals), their presidents or board of directors, or indeed on the strategic planning accomplishments and initiatives of any of the medical establishment. There is no where to even cast such a vote.

Canada's 100 billion dollar medical business is run like anything but a business! It is, however, a massive (bottomless until recently) insurance scheme, which pays off on all prepaid policy holders equally with no premium penalties. All policy holders pay the same premiums for young and old, healthy and unhealthy, self-abusive or not. All policy holders get the same coverage and the same care. What they do not get is 'red carpet' service.

When you go to the doctor's office, the clinic, the hospital or the ER, do they rush to assist you, show you a chair, get you a refreshment, and ensure that you are comfortable? No! It is not exactly like being waited on in an exclusive dress shop, car dealership or hotel. You are sick. You want and need help. You came for help. You check in, register and you wait! You wait with the rest of the 'herd'! In fact, it seems as though they may even be inconvenienced by your presence! The last thing they want is another 'customer'. What kind of 'business' is that? One hospital CEO once remarked that the only thing stopping him from creating the most efficient hospital in the country was the patients. They get in the way of hospital efficiency!

Hey ... Look At Me!

If none of these large organizations are putting the individual first, then how do you effect change in the system? The highest priority is currently placed on the large numbers of different patient populations, e.g. Cancer care, cardiac care, mental health, etc. The individual patient's priority is set by the doctor and nurse taking direct care of you at the time of your illness.

The Canadian government has been and continues to be involved in a massive re-assessment of the health care system which is currently estimated at costing the government and private agencies about 100 billion dollars per year. The problem is, they are still not even discussing (let alone focusing) on the individual. They can't! The individual patient is not even on their radar screen!

Some of the things that can be done by individuals to change the system are: writing to the editors of local papers, talking to the hospital's patient advocate (who is a hospital employee), calling a lawyer, or screaming at a nurse or doctor. However, none of these strategies seem to be effective. Even writing to the paper usually results in the predictable hospital response: *"we are doing the best we can with the limited financial resources we have, but will strive to do better in our pursuit of excellence!"* Which nicely translates to "leave your charitable donation for the capital building project in the lobby"!

As an individual, there are two very effective ways to create change in the health care system. First, you can vote for the political party whose view on health care is the same as yours. Hopefully if elected, they will follow through with their campaign promises. Secondly and most effectively, ensure that you get a high priority by actively participating in your own health care. Keep records, open good lines of communication and generate professional interest in your individual health life.

Keys To Surviving Admission To Hospital

Once the decision has been made to hospitalize you, there are many special arrangements that will need to be made quickly. It is always awkward being admitted to hospital, especially if the length of your stay is dependant on how rapidly you recover. From the time you enter the hospital, you will be referred to as a number. You will be the guy (or lady) in Room 4526. This is a difficult thing to get around, but you will have to make yourself noticeable, in order to not become one of the 'herd'! Remember, preparation and communication are at least 90% of the battle.

Preparation

It is not unusual these days to be 'on call', waiting at home until a bed becomes available in hospital. If by chance you are fortunate enough to have advanced warning of your hospitalization date (and aren't admitted directly from the emergency room), you can prepare.

To Do List

- Confirm your admission with the admitting department.
- Have someone take care of your children or pets.
- Ensure that all of your doctors are notified of your admission.
- Make sure they know the date and proposed length of stay.
- Tell them the reason that you are being admitted.
- Inform your workplace or school.
- Have someone re-book important meetings and appointments for you.
- Have someone check your mail and email.
- Cancel any travel plans that you won't be making.
- Have your newspaper subscription held until you are back.
- Set your lights on timers.
- Make all preparations you would if you were going away for a few weeks.

What To Bring

The following is a list of suggested things to bring to the hospital. Add your own items to the list.

Do Bring

- Kleenex and personal hygiene items
- Shampoo conditioner, and shaving supplies
- Soap and other toiletries (hairbrush, elastics)
- $20.00 (preferably in coins, for parking and vending machines)
- Small snacks and juice boxes (if permitted)
- Pyjamas / extra clothes (not your best!)
- Spectacles (reading glasses) or hearing aid
- *Copies* of identification
- Personal phone book
- Batteries
- Pen and paper
- Health card and personal health care diary
- Reading material, crossword books, deck of cards,
- Portable radio

What Not To Bring

Do not bring anything that you do not want to lose! Most hospitals are poor at finding misplaced belongings.

Do Not Bring

- Wallet!
- Original copies of identification!
- Jewelry!
- A lot of cash!
- Pets!

Bring your medications in their original bottles. Show them to the admitting nurse and the nurse that is assigned to you on your floor, but do not let them take your medication away. Often medications get misplaced. Instead, have a family member or friend take them home for you once you have shown them to the doctor and nurse. You do not want to keep them with you. Medication mistakes happen. Medications are often administered through intravenous (I.V. drip) and therefore, while you do not think you have received your regular medication, it may already be in your system. You must not take your own medication unless told to do so! Make sure you know the identification and purpose of all medication you are given and expected to take.

Getting In - It's Not That Easy!

It would not be unusual for your admission to have been delayed or cancelled more than once. When you do arrive at the hospital you should go to the admission area. Hopefully you have received directions on where it is located in advance. Be prepared to give them your personal I.D., your health card number, other insurance number, address, phone, next of kin, etc. Always use your full name. Many patients have the same last name. Make sure they get your date of birth correct. Check your ID bracelet and make sure it shows your name. If you are being admitted from the emergency department, the hospital will obtain the information required, and you will be transported directly to your room (eventually!).

At the admission desk, make certain to inform the admitting personnel of your wish to have your doctor notified of your admission to hospital. Request that their name be added to the admission documents to ensure that they receive a summary of your stay. After all, they know more about you than anyone in the hospital, and their input is critical. You should always call your doctor's office to inform them of your admission. It is important that the doctors who know you be involved in your hospitalization if you are to have continuity of care and understanding of your overall health issues. If you request the involvement of your personal physician, you will be recognized as a patient of a particular doctor rather than as an 'orphan' patient.

Give the following phone numbers to the admissions personnel; emergency contact, next of kin and power of attorney if you have one. Have your personal phone book with you so you can call friends, relatives, or physicians.

Your Hospital Room

On arrival, you will be interviewed by the ward nurse. She will take your blood pressure, temperature and complete a questionnaire. This is the time to ask questions!

★ ★ ★ ★ ★

"...Educated, well-informed, and demanding patients get better care than those who don't know what questions to ask or who have no one to ask the questions for them"

Dr. Carolyn Bennett
(2000) in <u>Kill or Cure? How Canadians Can Remake Their Health Care System.</u>

Questions To Ask

- When and how many visitors can I have?
- Are there specific limits on visitors (i.e. number at one time, children under 12 years old, family pets, etc.)?
- Is there a way to limit visitors if I want privacy?
- Is there a special rate for parking (daily or weekly flat rate)?
- Can someone move my car if it is in the emergency parking lot?
- When are meals served?
- Can I wear my own clothes/pyjamas? If not, why not?
- Where are the cafeteria, gift shop and vending machines?
- Can my family bring me food or treats? (Do I have a special diet?)
- Who do I give my advance directives to?

Special Requests

Ask

- Can I get a newspaper?
- Can I walk around?
- Can I leave the floor?
- Can I have a TV?
- Can I go outside?
- Can I have a drink- beer or alcohol?
  (Ask the doctor - not the nurse!).
- Can my wife or husband stay overnight?

There are probably more questions that you will have so don't be afraid to write them down. You should also ask the nurse about any concerns regarding food allergies, likes and dislikes, as well as any religious concerns you may have. Remember, you are not in prison! This is a hospital. You are a customer and you should be treated with respect! Hospitals are very conventional institutions. Many traditional habits and customs still remain. Don't be afraid to question what appears to be a holdover from a time gone by.

Dealing With Professionals

When you are admitted to hospital, you may be cared for by your personal physician if he has hospital privileges. If he doesn't you will be assigned a physician to take charge of your 'case' during your hospitalization; not a physician chosen by you or known to you. Make sure you know specifically who this professional is. Make sure he knows specifically who you are. Don't assume that they remember you from one day to the next. It is critically important that there is someone who is not only in charge but who will communicate with you and your family on a daily basis. Depending on the complexity of your problem, there may be many physicians involved. In this situation it is absolutely necessary that one of them act as your 'quarterback' and ensure communication among the physicians. This 'stranger' must know you well enough to make important diagnostic and treatment decisions that reflect your wishes. Be careful of your assumptions on professionalism; *trust not blind trust!* You should ask that your family doctor be consulted if there is any question regarding your health care to date.

There are numerous reasons why you may wish to request a transfer of your care to another physician. Some patients prefer either male or female physicians, younger physicians, older 'wiser' physicians, or those similar in culture or language. Some patients also prefer physicians with a different attitude or bedside manner. There is absolutely nothing wrong with making this request. Don't be embarrassed to discuss your request with the physician assigned to you. He likely will be surprised or even disappointed. Make sure he realizes that this is nothing personal. This change may take time if there is a shortage of physicians in your hospital. This sort of thing is not done frequently. The system of assigning a doctor to your care is for the convenience of the hospital, not you.

Requesting A Change Of Physician

- Tell the doctor assigned to you that you would prefer another physician.
- Ask that your care be formally transferred to another physician.
- Remember, the physician you choose must have hospital privileges.
- If you have a physician in mind, make them aware of your request.
- This process is different than obtaining a second opinion.
- If you would feel more comfortable, request the involvement of a specialist.

Restrictions placed on hospitalized patients are limited to those written by the doctor as orders on the chart. Some examples of these are: activities, visitors, diet, moving about the hospital and day passes. Should you want to request a day pass to go home and check on things, get your nurse to ask your doctor about it. If possible, you will want to know what time of day you may leave, how long you may be gone, and how often you can go. This may allow you some flexibility for your childcare plans or other arrangements that you have to make (such as feeding your pet). During your stay you will want to do the following to ensure that you get quality care and proper follow-up:

Keeping Yourself And Others Informed

- Wear a name tag. How else do you think they will recognise you!
- Write your name on a piece of paper or masking tape and attach it above your bed where everyone can see it clearly.
- Record the names of all professionals involved in your care.
- Have the doctor review and thoroughly explain all test results.
- They should also explain diagnoses and plans for treatment.
- Always ask questions and be sure that you get answers that you understand.
- If you don't understand, say so and ask for clarification.
- Ask the doctor what time of day he makes his rounds.
- Ask when your doctor will be in to see you.
- Ask what arrangements will be made if the doctor in charge will be away for an extended period of time (e.g. weekends).

You should be awake and alert when the doctor makes his rounds and be ready with your questions. Make arrangements to have your spouse or child/parent in attendance to participate in your discussion with the doctor.

Be aware: you share the responsibility of making sure they have the right patient!

There is no way that you will remember details such as names of physicians later on. Your personal physician will need this information to ensure appropriate follow-up care. Remember to I.D. yourself every time you interact with a doctor, nurse or technician. They are busy and cannot be expected to remember everyone's name. Mistakes are frequently caused by wrong identification.

Receiving Medication While In Hospital

Medications can be dangerous. Normally, when you receive a prescription from your doctor, it is explained to you individually and double-checked and explained a second time by a pharmacist. When you're in the hospital however, you are now one of 30 or more patients on the 'ward'. Despite all efforts, there remain many medication errors in hospitals. There are over 200 ways to make a medication error! Sadly, there have been many errors in administering medications to patients in hospitals which have resulted in serious harm and even death.

Be Careful! ! !

- Ask for a list of drugs prescribed for you and when they will be given.
- Ask for notification of any changes made to your prescriptions and why.
- Ask for a re-check of all medications before they are given.
- Don't take it unless you are sure.
- Tell each nurse your allergies (especially to food such as peanuts).
- Don't assume important information is transmitted from doctor to nurse or nurse to doctor.
- Weigh yourself daily and record it.
- Ensure your ID is checked - not just your *name* but check your *ID band* every time a drug is given to you!
- If you feel you are having a reaction after you take a medication tell the nurse right away!

★ ★ ★ ★ ★

"Each year, an estimated 10,000 patients die in Canadian hospitals as a result of staff errors, while a further 10,000 die from 'non-preventable adverse events' such as hospital infections and unexpected drug complications. Another 20,000 give or take, die of unforeseen or preventable causes while under care outside hospitals. That's an average of 100 people taken every single day"

Maclean's Magazine
December, 2002

★ ★ ★ ★ ★

Religious, Legal And Ethical Issues

You should find out if there is anyone who can inform you about your religious concerns. Ask if the hospital has a rabbi, minister, priest or chaplain who visits patients in the hospital. Ask when they visit. These people are not only there to deal with your religious concerns, but are also available to act as a shoulder to lean on and to lend a compassionate ear. Being hospitalized automatically puts people in a vulnerable position, amplified by illness. Acting out (anger, hostility, etc.) may be symptomatic of deeper emotions such as fear and anxiety. Find out if there is a chapel where you can perform your religious beliefs or ceremonies in private.

Ensure you inform the staff of your advance directives, desire not to be resuscitated, refusal of blood transfusion, and any other restriction you have placed on your care. The nurse will be of help. Ensure that your wishes are recorded on the 'active' hospital chart! You may want to contact your lawyer to prepare your power of attorney and review your will especially if you are critically ill or about to have a serious operation.

If you are not happy with the medical or nursing care, you should ask to speak with the Nurse Manager, the Nursing Director, your doctor or the patient advocate. All of these people should be able to help you find a solution to your problem. If you believe that there has been an error in your treatment, always notify the nurse and doctor as quickly as possible! It is important to tell them right away so they can take corrective measures to minimize consequences. If there is any resistance, ask to speak to the patient advocate. Nothing will change, nothing can be done unless a written letter of complaint is sent with a copy to the highest official (e.g. chief of medical staff, chief nursing officer, chief operating officer, or even chairperson of the board of trustees). If it isn't recorded, it didn't happen!

Every hospital should have a patient advocate. This person is there to help you if you wish to lodge a complaint about a doctor, staff member, procedure or treatment. They will also help you if you wish to express your thanks for terrific care. They can guide you in the rules regarding tipping or buying gifts for the staff. You may for example, wish to leave a donation to the fund-raising campaign.

Getting Out - Nothing's Easy!

Not that long ago, patients were admitted to hospital for even prolonged periods with relatively minor ailments. Today, the lengths of hospital stay have been reduced to the point that patients frequently feel they have been discharged too early. The most important aspect of being discharged from hospital is in the planning. Don't allow yourself to feel rushed. This step is just as important as being admitted but does not receive the same level of attention. This admission is but a short-term, problem-focused health care contract with the institution. The success of your stay requires that the events of your hospitalization be summarized and put into the context of your overall health care plan.

★ ★ ★ ★ ★

"Patients whose followup doctors receive a hospital discharge summary are less likely to need readmission"

Jenny Manzer
The Medical Post · March, 2002

Things To Do Before You Leave The Hospital - Professional

- Discuss the final diagnosis, test results and treatment plan with the physician in charge (make sure you clearly understand and take notes).
- Review all medications with the nurse or physician in charge.
- Find out who will be in charge when you leave the hospital? (e.g. your personal physician, nurse practitioner, specialist, etc.).
- Request that a copy of the discharge summary note be sent to your family doctor/specialist A.S.A.P. (It may never arrive!).
- Ask to take a brief written interim summary with you.

Always ask the doctor when he thinks you will be discharged. If it is a Friday for example and the doctor will not be in again until Monday, ask if you need to stay in hospital all weekend only to be released Monday morning. If your personal physician is not available to release you, can he phone in from his office and have the doctor on-call sign you out? There is no need to waste your valuable time or the health care system's money staying in the hospital because there is no one available to sign you out!

Things To Do Before You Leave The Hospital - Practical

- Know when you will be discharged from the hospital.
- Make all of the necessary arrangements for transportation.
- Arrange for help at home and nursing care if needed.
- Think about what groceries or medical supplies that you may need.
- Make sure you retrieve your valuables and medications before leaving.
- You will want to know if you will be discharged on a weekend so that you may get someone to buy your medical supplies before the weekend when the stores may be closed.

Arrangements

There will be many services that you will need to arrange in advance of your discharge from the hospital.

Arranging Services

- Nursing visits or home care visits
- Assistance around the house
- Social assistance
- Counselling
- Organizations that specialize in your illness
- Financial assistance (especially for devices such as walkers)
- Other forms of mental, physical and emotional support

When you are discharged from the hospital, you should inform your personal physician immediately. Give him the details of your treatment and tell him what tests were performed so that he may watch for the results. If your doctor's office knows what date you were released, they will probably know when to expect a final summary of your admission. Ask when you should follow-up to see if they have received your summary and test results.

Chapter Summary

- **Remember you are a stranger!**

- **In a large hospital you are but one of hundreds of patients!**

- **Make your personal preferences known in advance!**

- **This is a health care facility – not a prison!**

- **You need not feel intimidated – Be in charge!**

- **You are a client or a customer – not a captive!**

- **Plan going in – Plan coming out!**

- **If you don't want to forget it – WRITE IT DOWN!**

- **You can't be too careful with medication!**

- **Get in and out as soon as you can!**

- **Don't let them lose your glasses or dentures!**

- **Wear an I.d badge!**

- **Most hospitals do not share medical records!**

- **Don't assume that anything is remembered from a prior hospitalization!**

Keys To The Waiting Game

The funding of Canada's health care system necessitates the creation and therefore management of lists of patients waiting to have something done. Limited budgetary control of throughput allows only so many appointments, tests and procedures per year. If the demand for these services exceeds the budgeted supply, the waiting list will lengthen. If the demand for these services decreases (unlikely), the waiting list will shorten. By the same token, if the budget increases and the demand stays the same, the waiting list will shorten; simple medical economics. There are no preset maximum or minimum lengths to most waiting lists. When they get uncomfortably long and generate public attention, they may be shortened by juggling resources.

Patients wait (put into a holding pattern) to gain access to the care they need. One would like to think that patients on waiting lists are being treated fairly, equally, timely, and are monitored by a well-organized, foolproof system. This is an overstatement at best! They wait until the resources become available to manage their problem. It has unfortunately become tolerable for some people to wait many months or years to access some needed services. To survive the 'Canadian Waiting Game' there are a number of things patients should know.

How Does Waiting Work?

Waiting times are not standardized. Waiting can vary from province to province, region to region, town to town, hospital to hospital, specialist to specialist and perhaps most commonly from doctor to doctor. You can see how a patient with a particular medical problem can occupy a position on several sequential waiting lists. As a specialist in cardiovascular medicine, I have watched the waiting lists for heart surgery lengthen and shorten over twenty years. I have some examples to share and have no doubt that other areas of medicine have similar experiences. These examples are true and accurate. I live with them every day of my professional life!

Some years ago, I heard of a patient whose heart surgery was cancelled eleven times (eleven!!!) The patient died after finally having the operation. Each surgeon develops their own list of patients. Each surgeon has a designated share of operating room time. Each surgeon therefore has his personal list of patients awaiting surgery. A particular surgeon, (because of personal popularity, rumoured surgical results, special expertise or plain old availability), can have a very long waiting list. One of his equally talented colleagues may have a much shorter waiting list simply because no one knows. Although efforts are made to minimize these differences, they exist nonetheless. Though we would like to think that the time spent waiting is based purely on medical grounds, to believe so would be naive. There are many other factors that dictate waiting time.

Patients Are To Be Seen AND Heard!

In the business of medicine (e.g. heart disease for example) there are several types of waiting:

1) Waiting to see your personal physician
2) Waiting to see a heart specialist when referred by your doctor
3) Waiting for results of heart tests to decide if something has to be done
4) Waiting for a bed in the hospital for a test (e.g. angiogram)
5) Waiting to see a heart surgeon for an opinion as to your need for a heart operation
6) Waiting to be admitted to the hospital for the heart operation
7) Waiting to see your heart specialist or surgeon after your recovery for a final assessment
8) Waiting for rehabilitation

It becomes quite obvious, that if every doctor, office, test and procedure has a waiting list, the process of waiting can be long, lonely, difficult and complex! Delays and cancellations can occur at every step of the way. It is easy to fall between the cracks, be forgotten or even lost!

Wheeling And Dealing In The "Waiting Game"

- Always confirm your appointments at least once if not twice!
- If you are in a waiting room for a long time do not be afraid to ask how many patients are ahead of you.
- If you move, make them aware of your new address and phone number.
- Don't be afraid to be a polite but 'squeaky wheel'.
- Keep your doctor informed about your health status (if things worsen let them know!).
- Ensure you are on the right 'list' (e.g. elective vs. urgent)!
- Keep in touch with the wait list manager (if there is one).
- Offer to be available if there is a cancellation!
- Don't allow yourself to be cancelled more than once!

Make sure that you are seen *and* heard. Do not sit and patiently wait until you are beyond help to ask what is taking so long. Being patient can sometimes be dangerous! That is not to say that you need to be rude and demanding, but rather make certain that the people involved in your care know exactly how urgent your particular problem is and that you are ready to have your problem fixed as soon as possible.

The Danger Of 'Being Patient'

One wonders if the term 'be patient' originated in the health care system. The danger of being too patient is clear; waiting allows things to happen. Your health status can change. It can get worse; it can get better! I have had several patients wait so long for bypass surgery that they no longer wanted to get it done! Yes, I have had people deteriorate and even die while waiting. There are websites designed to inform you about Canadian waiting times and lists.

Waiting List Websites

- **The Western Canada Wait List Project** – (www.wcwl.ca) gives patients an idea of how they will be prioritized by including "priority forms".
- **The Fraser Institute** – (www.fraserinstitute.ca -then click on 'health') "waiting your turn". This is the Fraser Institute's annual report.
- **Statistics Canada Report on Access to Health Care Services** – (http://www.statcan.ca/Daily/English/020715/ d020715a.htm)
- Individual provinces each have websites devoted to surgical wait times, as do many hospitals.

This 'waiting game' can have profound effects on you. Maybe you are not well enough to work. Your family dynamic changes. You are bitter and depressed and more arguments occur in the household. Both you and your family are worried about what can happen. You feel alone. Thousands wait in the same way. The longer the wait, the more problems occur.

What You Should Know

Learn all of your options for treatment and do your research! Make sure the appointment or procedure is necessary. Some waiting lists, (not all) are monitored by professionals whose job it is to detect change and modify problems on the list. This doesn't always work. Most waiting lists are not monitored. You wait to be contacted without really knowing what's happening. Here too, you are one of many. You assume the system is fair. You assume the system is tightly controlled and reliable. Never make assumptions.

Questions For When You Are On A Waiting List

- What is the exact date for the appointment or procedure?
- Is this waiting time absolutely necessary (can someone else handle my case or perform the procedure)?
- Should I be prepared to go if there is a cancellation?
- How does this doctor's waiting list work?
- What can I expect?
- When and how often will I be notified?
- Who should I notify if my condition changes?
- How will my condition be monitored and by whom?
- Is there a list of things I need to know while on the waiting list?

Clarify all of your concerns about the waiting list. You are the one waiting. Your life is being disrupted. It's your health that will deteriorate. You are the only one who is monitoring your situation. You may be one of several hundred, but this one is *you*! This is one game in which you should be an active player and not waiting on the bench! Again...participation is the key.

Things To Help You Wait - For Those 'Little' Waits...

Sometimes you may find yourself sitting in a doctor's waiting room for a very long time (as any woman waiting to see a obstetrician has observed). There are several things you can do to make the experience less traumatic.

Making The Waiting Room Livable

- If you bring a child...bring toys, snacks, a bottle or juice, a crayon and a paper...most important - a change of clothes or a diaper!!!
- If you are alone, bring something that you like to read (rather than reading a magazine from 1975!).
- If you bring an elderly person bring juice, a newspaper you can read to them, and maybe a snack.
- Always bring your health care diary – you can use the waiting time to write down extra questions and update your files.
- Always bring a pen!
- Park somewhere that is not dependant on you putting money in the meter (the 'meter reader' will beat you to it every time!).
- Do not attempt to book another appointment the same day (you know you will never make it to the second one on time!).
- As the expression goes ... "pack a lunch". Relax...it always takes an hour longer than you think it will!

Whether you are waiting a few hours, a few weeks or a few months...the key to waiting is to be prepared, be persistent and communicate regularly with the people who book the appointments for you. Keep people informed about your status and be ready to go when called.

Are you visible in the herd?

Chapter Summary

- Know your treatment options!

- Are you and your doctor convinced you are on the right waiting list?

- How you present yourself dictates how quickly you will be seen!

- Don't assume your personal physician knows anything about the waiting list!

- Communication is critical!

- Educate yourself about the problem and the necessity of the appointment or procedure.

- Be prepared for a phone call.

- Learn to live your life in the meantime!

- Don't put everything on hold while you are on a waiting list. The waiting may go on for the rest of your life!

- Acting more sick than you are does not help you!

- Don't allow yourself to be cancelled more than once!!!

Keys To Diagnostic Testing

Now that the doctor has heard your description of the symptom, questioned you further, and performed an appropriate physical examination, he may arrange for certain diagnostic tests to confirm the diagnosis and define the extent of your problem. Testing should never replace a thorough patient history and physical examination!

These tests can be either simple or quite sophisticated. Tests such as blood samples, urine samples or x-rays are often referred to as routine. Others are much more sophisticated such as angiograms, CT scans, or MRI's. Each test is done to answer a specific question. If you know what the question is, then you know why the test is being performed. The refinement of the question and the number of tests often reflect your physician's clinical judgement.

Do not allow yourself to be put at unnecessary risk for the sake of curiosity! No test is completely safe. People faint having a blood test. In fact, you could have a car accident driving to the lab just for the test! Always remember that these tests are used to clarify the diagnosis not make it! Diagnostic tests are not designed to replace your doctor's training and clinical experience. They are designed to confirm his suspicions and improve the precision of the diagnosis. They are also used to monitor the effects of therapy. Don't be afraid to ask how reliable the results of the particular test are. (More about results later).

The Diagnostic Band Wagon

Diagnostic testing should never be assumed free of imperfections. There is always a chance that your results are incorrect or misleading. Murphey's Law states: "If it can go wrong it will go wrong", it's only a matter of time before it does!

Things That May Go Wrong

- Mislabelling
- Misfiled
- Wrong test performed
- Wrong patient tested
- Wrong name on requisition
- Wrong file, or chart
- Contaminated samples
- Under-qualified laboratory employees
- Equipment malfunction
- Result never received

There has been an exponential increase in the number of available diagnostic tests. Some patients and doctors believe that the more technology is used, the better. This is not always true. Frequently, patients are referred for a test that has a chance of causing serious harm even death. This can even occur when the doctor is almost certain the patient does not have the disease the test was designed to expose. If a test carries a potentially serious risk, it should only be performed on those patients who will definitely benefit from the result. Every test should be preceded by a weighing of the risks and benefits involved. This is a defining characteristic of good clinical judgment. Priority Patients ensure they are involved in this process. Don't confuse risk/benefit with cost/benefit!

Imagine using a jet to get to work when you live ten blocks away. Sometimes newer, faster and more expensive is not always better! Patients will hear the terms invasive and non-invasive when it comes to diagnostic testing. Examples of non-invasive tests include: ECG, chest x-ray. Invasive tests imply that the body is being entered by a tool or device (e.g. angiogram, biopsy). Generally speaking, invasive testing carries more risk and should be given more consideration. If the question is important enough and requires invasive testing so be it. If a non-invasive test is good enough, it should be done first. It's safer!

Do not feel you need to endure every available test to diagnose your illness. The complications of some tests are not immediately obvious (e.g. repetitive nuclear isotope studies (scans) allow accumulation of radiation effects). Tests can also be repetitive. You should not undergo two different tests if they both offer the same answer. If two tests are required, one should reflect a refinement of the answer to the first. Frequently, non-invasive tests are performed to either negate or confirm the need for an invasive test. More than one diagnostic test result may be required since frequently clinical problems are clarified by the answers to *several* questions.

Tests That Must Be Done Vs. Tests That May Be Done

It is inappropriate to investigate and treat all patients having the same complaint in the same manner. A particular test might be *absolutely necessary* in one patient whereas in another it may be *useful*. For example, a patient with typical angina (chest pain) *must* have a coronary angiogram before considering bypass surgery. On the other hand, a patient may present with a complaint of atypical chest pain. In this circumstance clinical suspicion *may* justify the performance of the test or it *may not*.

If the same test is done on all patients with the same problem or complaint, the question being asked is vague and not personalized. As an example, population screening with mammography is useful in detecting early breast cancer but also uncovers benign lesions that require further investigation. The question in this instance was not "Does the patient have cancer?" but rather "Does the patient have any breast abnormality that could be cancer?" Similarly, the presence of narrowed arteries on a coronary angiogram does not answer the question "What is the origin of the chest pain?". A patient can have chest pain from a hiatus hernia while her narrowed coronary arteries are causing no symptoms at all!

All new diagnostic tests are adopted with enthusiasm. When compared to currently available tests, any newly developed procedure should offer more precise answers. Be careful not to be too demanding of your physician when it comes to diagnostic tests. Priority Patients will appreciate the need for tests that *must* be done but require much discussion concerning those that *may* be done.

Special Preparations

Once you and your physician have determined that diagnostic tests are in your best interest, you need to be aware of what is required in preparation. Remember, always write down the details of when, where, and why you are having the test done. Here are some important questions to ask:

Questions To Ask About Diagnostic Tests:

- Do I need to dress in a special way?
- Should I book the day off work?
- Can I bring someone with me?
- Do I need to record my fluid intake?
- Do I need to fast before the test?
- Do I take my usual medications?
- Is there anything I should or should not do before the test?
- Is there a pamphlet outlining how to prepare for the test?
- Will I be sedated?
- Is it painful?
- Will I need assistance to get home after the test?
- How long does the test take?

Feel free to make a list of questions to ask your doctor and if necessary make a follow-up appointment before the test to clarify any lingering concerns.

Getting Your Results

Get the results of your tests as soon as possible and review them with your physician. It is the responsibility of the physician who ordered the test to ensure that he has seen the results. It is the patient's responsibility to ensure that the results are explained to them by the physician. If you know what the original question was, you are more likely to understand the answer. If you (the patient) haven't had the test result explained to you, has any one reviewed it? It is always more difficult to obtain any information after it has been filed away and forgotten. Don't be afraid to ask for a copy of the test result for your personal health diary. When I ask patients for their test results they frequently tell me they didn't receive them and therefore they must be normal. Do not assume that no news is good news! Results just like anything else, may be delayed, misplaced or forgotten.

Chapter Summary

- **The right diagnostic test can be extremely useful!**

- **Technical difficulties can occur with any test.**

- **Clearly identify yourself to the lab personnel.**

- **Know why you are having the test done.**

- **Know how the test result will affect your treatment. Choosing the right test requires a lot of thought (don't shoot birds with cannons)!**

- **Understand the risk. Is the test invasive or non-invasive?**

- **Not all diagnostic tests are completely safe.**

- **Don't have the test done simply because your friend did!**

Secrets Surrounding Therapeutic Options

Once you become involved in your health care, the complexity of decision-making quickly becomes apparent. It is always more simple to accept a one-sided decision made by your physician. Physicians are used to that. They may assume you do not want to participate in the decision making process. In fact, many of us don't want to make the big decisions that affect our health. We feel unqualified or incapable. How often have I heard, "You decide doc, you're the expert". As an experienced physician, my response (and now expectation) is that the patient and her family, with my help, will make the ultimate decision regarding her care. I inform them of the problem, the treatment options available, and what I believe to be the appropriate choice of therapy. I expect the patient and her family to seriously consider that information and direct me as to how they would like to proceed. To achieve this level of participation, patients must *acquire* a great deal of information regarding their options.

In medical decision-making, patients should realize there are important concepts which affect professional reasoning and action. If you appreciate the essence of these principles you have attended the equivalent of a 'medical school for patients' in which you develop an awareness of the driving forces behind much of today's health care. These concepts include:

- Appearance vs. Reality
- Reasonable vs. Excessive
- Appropriate vs. Necessary

What Are Appearances Anyway?

Appearance versus *reality* is a very difficult subject for patients. For example, when asked if you prefer an older physician with a great bedside manner who takes his time when making a diagnosis instead of a young doctor who rushes but uses all of the latest diagnostic tests and treatments possible, who would you choose? NEITHER! If the older physician lacks the current scientific knowledge and high-tech know how of his younger colleague, the comforting approach may look good but lack effectiveness. If the younger physician lacks wisdom in comparison to his older colleague, the scientific and high-tech approach may look good, but lack appropriateness if applied without the sensitivity gained from years of clinical experience.

One may also be misled in the diagnostic process. It is well known that a woman presenting with a complaint of chest pain has about a 35% chance of having a positive exercise test, apparently indicative of underlying heart disease. However, many of these are false positive tests in patients who appear to have heart disease but in fact, do not. Enlightened health care consumers realize that, as in any other business, reality is subject to perception.

Made To Measure vs. Off The Rack!

Sometimes treatment options are *reasonable* and sometimes they can be *excessive*. You may be presented with a treatment option that seems excessive or unreasonable. For example, your doctor suggests that your 85-year-old mother have coronary bypass surgery, a treatment he suggests in most patients. She is not currently badly disabled and a trial of medication has not yet been attempted. Her risk of death at surgery is significant. Medication would pose less risk, ease her discomfort and you believe would be more reasonable. Given the absence of a right or wrong treatment option in this case, the patient should realize the therapeutic approach should 'fit' the specific situation. Yes, the treatment can be worse than the disease!

It is not unreasonable to request a description of other available treatment options. Your doctor's suggestion is just that – a suggestion. If for example, your teenager is prescribed a cholesterol-lowering drug because her blood cholesterol level is a little high, and there are no indications that she will develop premature heart disease, you might consider this excessive treatment. A more reasonable approach might be a low-fat diet and exercise. Enlightened health care consumers realize that good care is customized.

If The Shoe Fits....

It is also important to differentiate between what is *appropriate* and what is absolutely *necessary*. This may have a great deal to do with the issue of informed consent. This concept forces you to realize that much of the advice and counsel you receive regarding the investigation and treatment of your problem is just advice! What is absolutely necessary is something that must be done. What is appropriate is something that can be or even should be done, but does not have to be done. For example, you have a gallbladder with a gallstone. You get the occasional discomfort after meals, but that is all. Your doctor advises you to have the gallbladder surgically removed. Is it absolutely necessary? No. Is it appropriate? Sure. Your discomfort may improve or you could have a complication in surgery!

Some medical treatments are so effective and well established that there is no question about the decision to apply them. They are scientifically accepted and the benefits to all patients with the similar complaint are proven beyond doubt. Unfortunately, most issues in medicine are not so straightforward. Certain forms of diagnostic testing and certain therapies are much less well proven in terms of their real value. Some tests are done to assist in the management plan. Some treatments are given in the hope that they will be of help or at least minimize complications.

Such interventions could be referred to as appropriate, but are they necessary? Occasionally physicians will strongly recommend a certain treatment causing patients to believe that it is absolutely necessary. In fact it may not be. For example, an orthopedic surgeon might make quite a convincing argument that a child needs corrective surgery for their hips (based on the projection of future problems), when in fact the child may grow out of the condition. The surgeon is recommending an appropriate surgical intervention that is not absolutely necessary. Enlightened health care consumers expect treatment to match their disease!

No Exchanges - No Refunds!

Decisions must be made. There are usually several options. Either participate in the process or let the health care team make all of the choices for you. If you let them decide for you, you must accept the outcome without anger or malice. When you are asked to sign a consent form, you are agreeing to the treatment and implying that you understand the test or treatment and all of its consequences. You are saying that you accept the risks, you understand the problem and agree knowingly to the plan of treatment! You share the responsibility of what follows. By participating in the decision making process, you truly are informed. You know the choices and recognize their limitations. If you must bear responsibility, let it be the responsibility for your action not your inaction. Don't be caught after the fact, wishing you had given it more thought or had been more involved.

It takes a fairly intelligent person to understand therapeutic options in medicine. Making such choices is not easy. After all the explanations, patients still say, "Just do what you have to". This would be the same as telling the barber to give you any haircut, the car salesperson to pick the model they like, or the dentist to fill the tooth or pull it – whatever they prefer! It is absolutely necessary that patients have faith in their health care team. Your faith should be in their skill to do their jobs well, not in their ability to make life choices for you without your input!

It is not necessary that your faith be blind or ignorant!

Keys To Preparing For Surgery

Surgery of any kind can be a frightening experience; it is especially difficult if you are not mentally and physically prepared. There are many things you can do to have a positive experience with a good outcome. We assume that you and your surgeon/partner have had an in depth discussion outlining the need for the surgery and the potential risks and benefits to you. If you haven't, do so before proceeding. Knowing exactly what to expect beforehand minimizes the chances of any surprises.

Before Proceeding - Surgical Vocabulary

Some operations are performed under emergency circumstances, prior to which it is very difficult to undertake prolonged explanations. These are usually preceded by a statement of the risks involved. You really have little choice. Elective (pre-planned) operations on the other hand allow plenty of time for discussion and informed decision-making.

There are two concepts you should be aware of concerning the indication (rationale) for the operation. The first and most obvious is to relieve a complaint such as pain, bleeding, or infection; a *therapeutic* operation. The second and less obvious indication for surgery is to minimize the potential for a complication occurring in the future; a *prophylactic* (preventive) operation. For example, a patient with disabling angina would have bypass surgery to relieve pain. A different patient with minimal angina but severely blocked arteries in the heart would have the surgery performed not to relieve pain but to decrease the risk of future heart attack.

These days most operations are performed at relatively low-risk to the patient in terms of both *morbidity* (non-fatal complication) and *mortality* (death). High-risk operations are those that are done with the full knowledge of both the patient and the physicians that the potential for morbidity and mortality is higher than is usually expected. When you are asked to sign a consent form prior to surgery, you confirm your knowledge of the operation and its associated risks.

Certain types of operations can only be performed in specialized medical centres or hospitals. These institutions have the necessary professional expertise and diagnostic surgical resources required for operations such as heart valve replacement, brain surgery and organ transplantation. Most other operations are routine, still requiring surgical expertise but less specialized resources such as gallbladder removal.

The Basics

Prepare in advance for your operation and recovery both in hospital and at home. Make arrangements for tasks that must be done. Recruit friends and family to help you. Delegate responsibilities before you go for surgery. Be sure that you are going to be able to rest undisturbed when you come home.

Preparations For Hospitalization:

- Picking up children (from school, etc.)
- Picking up the mail
- Checking your e-mail
- Paying bills
- Watering plants
- Feeding pets
- Taking out the garbage
- Household maintenance

Making arrangements for your hospitalization is only part of the challenge. You must also prepare for the period of time you are home but unable to perform your usual duties during your convalescence. You may require special home care services or equipment. Some things you might want to do in advance include:

Preparing For Recovery At Home:

- Arrange for any special assistive devices.
- Arrange for nursing services.
- Arrange your home so that you may get around easily once you return.
- Prepare your meals in advance and keep them in the freezer (you may not want to cook when you get home).
- Update your health care diary (including all lab test, x-rays, etc.).
- Get your insurance issues in order (disability, critical illness, additional hospital coverage, etc.).
- Prepare legal documents, especially your advance directives.
- Name your power of attorney if you so wish.
- Don't forget to advise your employer how long you will absent.

Preparing Yourself

Be certain that you have asked all of the important questions before consenting to any surgery. You should always ask the following:

Questions To Ask Before Surgery:

- Is the surgery absolutely necessary?
- Is this the correct surgery to have?
- Will this surgery cure you or simply relieve symptoms?
- Does this particular surgery have to been done right now?
- Where and how big will the incision be?
- What is the surgeon's success rate with this procedure?
- What are the risks involved?
- How long does the operation take and who will be present?
- Will one surgery be enough to correct the problem?
- What should you expect when you wake up?
- Should you donate blood in advance in case they need to use it during surgery?
- What are the possible complications or side effects from the anesthetic?
- Who will be the physicians in charge of my care?
- Do you need to know if I am pregnant?

Find out about all nutritional, medicinal, and behavioural issues that you should be concerned about before your surgery.

Other Questions To Ask Before Surgery:

- Should I take my medications the day of the surgery?
- Should I eat before the surgery?
- What vitamins, pain killers or other over-the-counter remedies can I take, and how long can I take them before surgery?
- What foods, herbs, vitamins or pain relievers will interfere with my recovery (some herbs can interfere with anesthesia and some herbs and vitamins can interfere with blood clotting)?
- Will regular drug and alcohol use (if this applies to you) affect your anesthesia or surgery? - Be honest, as it can sometimes affect how responsive you are to anesthetics!

✱ ✱ ✱ ✱ ✱

When having an amputation, it has been suggested that you write with a permanent marker "wrong arm" or "wrong leg" on the limb that is not to be removed for an added measure of security.

Judith Blake
Seattle Times, January 5th, 2000

Yet more ideas for smoothing out the recovery process at home:

Additional Help For Recovery At Home

- Have someone at home with you to cope with visitors when you need more sleep.
- Have a friend or family member check on you periodically.
- Make arrangements to be on vacation.
- Have someone care for your small children for a while, as seeing you with tubes or in a weakened state might be somewhat disturbing for them.
- Find out about any exercises that you may do to help recovery or maintain proper blood flow.
- Make sure you have a hot water bottle or ice pack (depending on what is necessary).
- Get pain prescriptions filled in advance if possible so that they are waiting for you when you get home.

Things To Bring To The Hospital

The following list of items should not be brought to hospital, such items can go missing!

Don't Bring:

- Wallet!
- Original copies of identification!
- Jewelry!
- A lot of cash!
- Pets!
- Fragrances!

The following is a list of things to bring to the hospital when admitted for your surgery. This list is not exclusive; bring what you feel is necessary. If you are unsure of whether or not you are allowed to bring an item, call the hospital and ask.

Things To Bring:

- Comfort items such as flowers, photos, religious medallions or beads
- Notepad and pencil
- Quilt, pillow, pyjamas
- Tissue and any other personal hygiene supplies
- Shampoo, conditioner, shaving supplies, soap and other toiletries (hairbrush and other accessories)
- $20.00 (preferably in coins, for parking and vending machines)
- Reading material, crossword books, deck of cards
- Files or other paperwork (you will finally have the time to do your taxes!)
- Small snacks and juice boxes (if permitted)
- Walkman/Discman
- Earphones for television
- Health card and personal health care diary
- *Copies* of identification
- Personal phone book

The Three R 's

The most important thing you have to do is trust others. Every hospitalization puts you in a vulnerable situation. You need to depend on your family, friends, the surgical team and other professionals. If you are used to being the organizer and the pillar that everyone else leans on, this will be a difficult time. Remember, this may not be the appropriate time to quibble over small details. Those trying to help you are doing their best. It is time for you to rest, relax and repair yourself.

Rest...

Relax...

Recover

Chapter Summary

- Don't forget to read the chapter on hospitalization!

- Satisfy yourself regarding the necessity of your surgery.

- Your signature on the *informed consent* implies you are informed!

- Be prepared and everything will run much more smoothly.

- Be prepared to deal with pain.

- Do not feel obligated to your visitors – they can be both a help and a hindrance.

- Although you expect a positive outcome, you must be prepared for the unexpected.

- Allow others to help you.

- Before surgery everyone worries about a possible complication. Afterwards no one expected it to happen!

Introduction To Knowledge And You: The Medical School For Patients

I believe that patients occupy a most intimate position and play the most pivotal role in their health care. I recognize and respect your position but I want you to realize how responsible you must be as a health care consumer, particularly during periods of frightening vulnerability. Most patients adopt a passive stance when exposed to the medical and nursing 'authorities', surrendering their individuality, assuming a psychological 'fetal position'. They endure waiting lists, abrupt behaviour, terse commentary, dogmatic instruction, unexplained strategies for 'care', unusual professional personalities, enforced hospital dress codes and frequent medical errors. In short, an overall dehumanization and 'herd mentality'.

Why does the medical establishment condone this type of behaviour from patients? Historically, it was only doctors who possessed the knowledge of the 'healing arts'. Treatments were relatively ineffective and patients were ignorant of health care issues. Doctors employed a large ceremonial component to diagnosis and therapeutic intervention. This evolved into a very authoritarian medical establishment. Doctors' new found 'paternal' authority commanded patient compliance but unfortunately perpetuated patients' ignorance of health care issues.

Perhaps we are in the final period of patients' submissive behaviour given the explosion of knowledge available to everyone plus the tremendous increase in expectation of 'successful' outcomes from all forms of treatment. Society's expectations of the medical establishment have grown exponentially. There are those who have become intolerant of medical errors and unsuccessful treatments. Others remain trapped in the not so critical past. We find ourselves in a confused period of high expectation leading to increasing medical-legal conflict. Yet, patients remain largely ignorant of fundamental health care issues. In the absence of meaningful patient participation in their own health care, it is difficult to identify the source of such high expectations. Perhaps the establishment has promised more than it can deliver. Paying your taxes and health insurance premiums neither confirms immortality nor advances your knowledge.

Getting Involved

Assuming you bought this book and assuming you have read everything to this point, you have already begun the process of getting involved. You have demonstrated an interest in advancing your knowledge of the health care system and how it works. You obviously care about yourself. You recognize the need for more personal involvement and active participation in your health life. Consider yourself enrolled in the first year of your 'personal medical school'. You represent the beginning of a transformation from the period of medical ignorance to the period of expanding patient education and awareness. You have high expectations of the system but you have even higher expectations of yourself and recognize the need for a partnership with the system. Excellence in your health care can only be achieved when you and the system recognize your responsibilities to one another.

Attending a 'Medical School For Patients' is an excellent place to begin. Your medical school is what you want it to be. Indeed it has to be customized to your individual needs. You will design your own independent learning to replace classes and lectures on topics that pertain to your interests. You will become street wise in your health care. Diabetics will become educated in all aspects of diabetes management. Patients with high blood pressure will learn about their medications and even become skillful in measuring their own blood pressure. Those of you with risk factors for developing heart disease will pursue education regarding preventive strategies: smoking cessation, weight loss, cholesterol lowering, blood pressure control, etc. These are very personal health care issues that only your behaviour can accomplish. The successful student will blend the advice of their health care team with personal disease management. They gain both knowledge and control of their health life and move towards obtaining their own personal health degree.

It's up to you. Indeed you may have to guide your health care professionals into this new era. Many of them are already there, but many of them are 'en route'. You already bear a number of medical responsibilities. The health problems you have are yours. If you are sick, it's up to you to seek help, to fill a prescription, to take your medication and to follow the advice of your physician. It's also up to you to know why you are doing this! The final year student in this personal medical school recognises the significance of decision-making. Ultimately, every decision made about your health care is yours. You sign off on what is called *informed consent*. You incorporate your knowledge of the problem, the therapeutic options available to you and the suggestions of your health care team, and then YOU CHOOSE.

Making A Contribution

By now, you have some idea of how the patient can be either a tremendous help or a gigantic burden to the health care system. Your active participation represents much more value than you can possibly imagine. Anything you can do to improve efficiency, communication and transfer of information can profoundly improve the system. By being your own advocate and assuming some responsibility for your health affairs, you become involved as a partner in the business of medicine. Simply recording the details of your symptoms and keeping a health care diary can save time for your doctor and money for the system. In this new era, patients will be expected to contribute in a number of ways; the Priority Patient will be creative in doing so.

Without the contribution of solid patient participation, no health care system in the world can survive. We do not have to continue to perpetuate the myth that the health care team is disconnected from the patient. In fact today, the patient is one of the most important members of this team. In the future, it will no longer be necessary for patients to seek the assistance of third parties to achieve equality. Hence the need for the patient to be enlightened, confident, and empowered. We are evolving but fail to recognize our changing identity as equal partners. More patients need to enrol in their own personal medical school. It will be interesting to observe the evolution and response of the other members of the health care team as patients assume their expanded responsibilities.

"We are rapidly coming to the point where we are starting to trust tests more than our own clinical judgment"

Dr. Richard Gruneir

The Medical Post • November, 2002

"There is a need to change medical culture and foster more consideration of the appropriateness of medical interventions ...physicians must reconsider the notion that just because something can be done, it should be done"

Dr. Charles Wright

Canadian Medical Association Journal • June, 2002

Secrets Of Interpreting Test Results

When faced with a patient's symptom or complaint, doctors begin their task by asking questions in order to clarify details in the patient's history. This is followed by the performance of a physical examination of the patient. During the examination, attention is paid to those parts of the patient's body most likely associated with the complaint. Other routine information is also obtained (e.g. blood pressure, temperature, etc.). With this information, the physician arrives at what is known as a 'working diagnosis', a preliminary suspicion as to the cause of the problem. The next step in the diagnostic process may be to entertain a 'trial of therapy': test a particular treatment for a short period of time to see if it works. More likely, the doctor will order one or more diagnostic tests that are designed to confirm their suspicions. Information obtained from the history and physical examination is extremely important in guiding this process. For example, a complaint such as chest pain, when interpreted in different ways, could trigger the performance of various tests, depending on whether the chest pain appears related to lung, heart, digestion, etc. It's all in the details!

Why Do They Order The Tests They Do?

Diagnostic tests are used for different reasons. Depending on the complexity of the clinical problem (symptom), one or more tests may be required to answer the question or questions being asked. Some tests are better used in combinations. A diagnostic test done in the absence of a good history and physical examination can be dangerous. I believe it was Woody Allen who once asked, "I have an answer, does anybody have a question?" If you don't know the question, it is difficult to know what to do with the answer! Any test result may have vastly different meaning depending on the clinical situation to which it is being applied.

Why Are Diagnostic Tests Ordered?

- Confirm a clinical suspicion
- Check organ function
- Monitor disease improvement or progression
- Monitor the effect of a treatment
- Assess patient for degree of disability
- Screen for a particular disease entity
- Clarify another diagnostic test result

Test Result - What Does It Really Mean?

Once the test has been performed, the result must be both read and interpreted. *Reading* the test (putting the results into words) is frequently done by machine, but may be done by a technician or any physician. *Interpreting* the test (placing the results into the context of the individual clinical situation) is an extremely important task performed by the patient's personal physician. This process should be guided by the original question.

Some tests are simply reported as *positive* (meaning the test result implies the existence of an abnormality) or *negative* test (which implies the absence of an abnormality). Some examples of these are: pregnancy test, blood in the stool, ketones in urine, spot on chest x-ray, etc. Some tests are reported with reference to a *normal range*. The results are either above, below or within the normal range of values. Some examples are: blood sugar level, hemoglobin, cholesterol, body temperature, etc. Increasingly complex tests generally require the results to be given in more *descriptive* language. Some of these are: CT scans, MRI, angiogram, ultrasound, etc.

The Objective Interpretation (Good And Bad!)

It is vital that the test results be interpreted by the physician responsible for initiating the process and caring for the particular patient. In this process, the doctor integrates test results with the history and physical examination to confirm the working diagnosis. If it is a fit, the diagnosis remains. If there is no fit, the working diagnosis could change. You can see the importance of understanding that the test result is only one piece of a complex puzzle. Acting on a test result without putting it into the context of the particular patient is dangerous. While this may sound confusing, it is the most critical component of the diagnostic process.

These examples are common. They occur frequently. You now realize that the test result must be interpreted in the context of the particular patient. You also realize that without a good history and physical examination, it is impossible to know which tests to order. If a test is done inappropriately or without a specific question in mind, the results can be very confusing (even to the educated)! The answer can be difficult to interpret. A good doctor asks good questions and knows what to do with the answers!

Here are two examples of situations requiring individualized interpretation of a test result:

1) A 62-year-old man, smoker with high blood pressure, high cholesterol, and normal physical examination experiences typical angina pectoris (heart pain) on exertion. His treadmill exercise test demonstrated poor physical condition and chest pain but was interpreted as a negative test implying there is no heart problem. This result should be considered a potential *false* negative test in view of the likelihood that he does have heart disease.

2) A healthy 35-year-old woman experienced atypical chest pain at rest. Her physical examination was normal and no heart murmur was heard. The cardiac ultrasound test reported severe mitral regurgitation (leaky valve). This result should be considered a false positive given the absence of symptoms and signs.

Go Hunting For Bears Where Bears Live!

Diagnostic tests tend to obey certain 'laws of chance'. The person ordering the test and subsequently acting on the result needs to appreciate these laws or principles. One of these rules is known as BAYES THEOREM. Don't go fishing where there are no fish! Don't hunt for bears where bears don't live! It sounds like simple common sense. It is, but oh how often it is forgotten. Do you think it is worth while looking for something in a place where it is not likely to be? Would you go shopping for groceries in a clothing store? Would you expect to find clothing for sale in a car dealership? Of course not! Now you are starting to appreciate this very simple principle.

If you do go hunting for bear in a location where bears don't live, and you think you see a bear, there is a good chance that what you are looking at is not a bear (*false positive*). It looks like a bear. It sounds like a bear. It walks like a bear but it is likely not a bear. It is a bear-look-a-like. If a test is ordered on a patient who is not likely to have the problem that the test is designed to uncover, the test will probably show that the patient does not have the disease (*true negative*). If the test suggests that the patient might have the disease, it is quite likely that the test is wrong (*false positive*). If a test is done on a patient very likely to have the disease the test is designed to find and the test is positive, the patient likely has the disease (*true positive*).

No one should perform diagnostic tests on patients who are unlikely to have the problem that the test is designed to uncover! What does this all mean? How can it possibly have anything to do with you? An exercise stress test done on a perfectly healthy, asymptomatic, young football player is expected to be 'normal' because the likelihood of him having heart disease is very small. If the test comes back positive and suggests that he has heart disease, it is more probable that the test itself is a *false positive*. The test is not accurately defining the true status of the patient's health.

An echocardiogram done on a perfectly healthy young woman with few or no symptoms is also expected to be 'normal'. If the echo shows severe mitral regurgitation and the patient does not have a heart murmur, it is likely that the leak is not as significant as the test might suggest.

These are examples of test results that do not fit the clinical situation. While this can happen, it is important to differentiate and understand the fact that test results (the reading) can be wrong; so too the doctor's assessment of the problem might be incorrect (the interpretation). Tests can be misinterpreted and disease can be silent! An abnormal test result does not necessarily mean that there is disease present! Nor does a normal test always mean that there is no disease! Many patients are referred to me simply to reinterpret the meaning of their test results.

Terminology We Should ALL Understand...

So you've had a test done and the results come back *abnormal* or positive. What should you and your doctor be considering? Were you expecting the test to be positive? If so, the test is confirming the working diagnosis. You are now more likely to have the disease. If you were doing the test to rule out the disease (you were expecting it to be negative), you are now faced with the problem of deciding whether you have the disease, a false positive result or another problem that looks like the disease you were looking for. You now require further testing to clarify what really is going on. If the second test confirms the findings of the first, there is now an even greater likelihood you have the disease. If the second test (a better test), does not confirm the findings of the first, it is much less likely you have the disease.

Accuracy is another term you may come across. It is the measure of precision of the test in comparison with other tests. A test may be very accurate when employed in a scientific study, but less than ideal when used under 'field conditions' (i.e. in the real world). For example, in my experience, nuclear studies on the heart are not as reliable as the medical literature suggests. Some test results are reported with a range of normal results. The concept of a range of normal is an effort to describe and quantify the range of values that exist among individuals believed to be disease free. The normal range of most tests is set to include 95% of disease-free people, leaving 2° % above and 2° % below (outside), the normal range. These people are disease-free, but their test is abnormal. By definition, 5% of the population has test results that are outside of the 'normal' range on any particular test.

Now you realize that *abnormal* and *diseased* may not be the same! The opposite is also true. Some individuals with disease will have test results in the 'normal' range. These are called *false negatives*. Note: Having an abnormal test does not mean that you have the disease, but it may increase the likelihood that you have the disease.

What's It All About Then????

Patients do the best they can to describe their symptoms. Frankly they are not always particularly good at this because they're not trained to do so. Doctors obtain histories from patients in a variety of environments and sometimes under difficult circumstances. Occasionally these histories are too brief and incomplete. Diagnostic testing may then be done under less than ideal circumstances created by inadequate communication, by misunderstanding and through the lack of a crystal clear question to be answered by the test. You can see why communication is the priority for both patients and doctors.

It is well known that diagnostic tests are imperfect in their ability to completely and accurately include or exclude disease. It is less well appreciated that the process of ordering, reporting and interpreting these tests can have a far greater impact than the test itself. It is certainly more comforting to think that technology is infallible and can predict the future as well as describe the present. The unfortunate truth is that occasionally test results are misleading and blindly acting on results can cause problems.

Priority Patients participate in the selection and ordering of their diagnostic tests. They are comfortable that the tests being performed seem reasonable, and they fully understand the question being asked. It is a given that they will discuss the test results with some knowledge. The best and most thorough physicians rely heavily on their patients to tell them all the necessary details in order to pursue the right course of action. They are good listeners. They realize the importance of an accurate history. They know the limitations of the process and practice the art and science of medicine.

"It must be appreciated that the history remains the richest source of information concerning the patient's illness...Perhaps more importantly, a careful history allows the physician to evaluate the impact of the disease, or the fear of the disease, on the various aspects of the patient's personality, affect, and stability"

Dr. Eugene Braunwald
"Examination of the patient" in <u>Heart Disease</u>
(a textbook of cardiovascular medicine)

2+2=13

(say what????)

"Medicine is an art - not always an exact science!"

RSB

Secrets Of The Numbers Game

Most research study results reported in the media are from what are called phase III studies. These usually involve several thousand patients and are conducted to see if a new form of treatment is better than current best practice.

Significance - What Does It Mean?

In the days before we had good antibiotics, people usually died from bacterial pneumonia. Today, a study looking at the effectiveness of penicillin would not require more than a hundred or so patients. Half of the participants would be given penicillin and half given a placebo (looks the same as penicillin but does nothing for the infection). There would be so many patients who received the penicillin that survived, and so many that received placebo and died, that the result would be obvious. In other words, if no previous effective therapy existed, any new *effective* therapy will require very few patients to prove the point. There was little need for statistical analysis since the results were so blatantly obvious.

Most new therapies today are designed to replace existing effective therapies because they are felt to be superior. So now, it is the incremental benefit (statistical significance) and cost of the newer treatment that decides if it is worth changing. Studies designed to show these new treatments are more effective must be larger and hence require many more research subjects. For mathematical (statistical) reasons, you must study large numbers of patients in order to show that a small difference between two similar treatment groups is 'statistically significant' or numerically important. The difference between two study groups is decided by the number of end points or events observed in each. If a 20% reduction in events is required to demonstrate superiority, it may take a very large number of events to find this 20%. Only at this level of scientific investigation can one find 'statistical' significance.

Clinical relevance (will the individual patient be better off?) is different from statistical significance. Here we need to understand the terms *relative* and *absolute*. A study could demonstrate a 33% difference between two groups being studied. This is a 33% relative difference. For example: A study with 100 patients in each of two groups 'revealed' a 33% relative reduction in mortality. That could mean there were 9 deaths in the placebo group and 6 deaths in the treatment group for a 33% reduction.

However, you quickly realize that the absolute difference between the two groups is only 3 patients, or a 3% absolute reduction in mortality! It is very easy to see why it is much more attractive to report a 33% relative reduction rather than a 3% absolute reduction in mortality. In the group that did not get the new treatment 9 died. Assuming all 100 patients in the test group that were given the new treatment took it, 9 would have died but only 6 actually died; 3 survived because of the new treatment. The other 91 patients in that same group took the treatment and were exposed to all of the potential side effects and complications but with no obvious benefits. In this trial, the 'number needed to treat' was 100 patients in order to demonstrate the benefit to 3 patients!

Significance - What Does It Mean To You?

Let's consider the example of a large contemporary clinical trial. In this hypothetical study of 20,000 patients (not unheard of today), a 33% reduction in mortality implies that 1/3 fewer patients suffered an end point (e.g. death) in the treatment group as compared to the control group (relative reduction in mortality). Depending on the number of deaths that occurred in the trial, 33% could represent a larger or smaller number of individual patients.

Relative vs. Absolute Outcomes (20,000 patient study)

		(Reduction)	
Group A	Group B	Relative	Absolute
900/ 10, 000 died	600/ 10, 000 died	33%	300
90/ 10, 000 died	60/ 10, 000 died	33%	30
9/ 10, 000 died	6/ 10, 000 died	33%	3

This chart demonstrates that a 33% relative reduction in mortality can translate into as many as 300 out of 20,000 benefiting or as few as 3 out of 20,000 benefiting from the new treatment. Is it a benefit to society if the other 9,997 (or even 9,700) patients have to take a treatment with all of the attendant risks, to help 3 (or even 300) patients? Some would find this a bit excessive and certainly very expensive. Perhaps this is why physicians will vary in their interpretation and practical application of results of scientific studies. By the way, no one knows in advance which patients are going to benefit and no one knows which patients will suffer complications from the intervention. Obviously, we are all searching for the patients at highest risk to receive the treatment. Low risk patients are much less likely to benefit. This is why there are so many people being treated with the latest medications. It also clearly explains that the treatment is not 100% effective since there is only a 33% reduction in risk. The Priority Patient will be involved in decisions regarding perceived benefits to her as an individual.

How Big Is This Game?

Millions of patients are involved in medical research and clinical trials. We thank them all for their volunteerism and active participation. We sincerely hope this reflects their concern about all aspects of their health care. Millions if not billions of dollars are spent on medical research every year. This financial support comes from government, private associations, generous benefactors and individual citizens. It must be remembered that large amounts of money donated in the name of research is also used in the process of patient education, information dissemination, and new strategies for delivering health care.

Even more financial investment in research comes from the medical products and pharmaceutical industries. New products and drugs studied scientifically and proven successful can have a massive market potential and therefore create huge profits for these industries. Although the amount of money invested in research sounds staggering, it pales in comparison to the profits on sales.

Medical Research - Sales And Marketing

Doctors and patients want to give and receive the best possible treatment to obtain the best possible outcome in every clinical situation. New drugs and devices carry the promise of better treatment results with fewer side effects compared to those currently available. Successful new discoveries are perhaps too quickly introduced to the market place. This is done with enthusiasm by the companies who developed them and the medical professionals who actively participated in the research efforts. Other medical professionals quickly subscribe to the prevailing wisdom and begin using these new products on their patients. At this point it is also a given that most physicians recommending the new therapy will discuss 'relative' not 'absolute' benefits with their patients.

The marketing strategies and advertising materials generally take full advantage of the relative reduction in mortality or other end points measured in the clinical trials. It is seldom for these strategies to promote the absolute reduction figures as they are usually far less impressive. The amount of money spent on these and other influential strategies is awesome. Companies will offer free products to physicians and institutions as incentives. Millions of dollars are spent on drug samples alone.

The results of scientific trials have become increasingly important to physicians and surgeons in their quest for improved treatments and better outcomes for their patients. In this regard, the medical establishment has witnessed/introduced a new trend in the application of research trial results. It is now expected that doctors should have evidence for the treatment options they choose in dealing with their patients. This new 'Evidence Based Medicine' movement now permeates the entire medical professional world. This new ideology, when applied with its original intent, motivates physicians to be aware of new knowledge and to apply it to their patients when appropriate. The manner in which a physician adopts this ideology will determine how he interprets and uses the results of the study. He will either apply this new data to all of his patients or hand pick the individuals under his care who he feels will most likely benefit from its application. How the scientific evidence is presented can be even more influential than the evidence itself. Frequently, the senior scientific investigators are the most ardent promoters of the study results. It takes an extremely confident and self-assured physician to personally evaluate the merits of each study and individualize treatment based on potential risks and benefits. It is far too easy to offer new therapies to all patients simply to satisfy an aggressively promoted ideology. Priority Patients understand exactly the purpose of their treatments.

Keys To Participating In Research Trials

It is possible that at some point you or a family member will be asked to participate in a research study. Modern medicine would not have advanced to where it is today without scientific research trials or "studies". Doctors have learned a great deal about medications and other treatments thanks to patients who were willing volunteers for the advancement of knowledge. The benefit to the doctor is his involvement in advancing medicine thus helping future patients. There is no guarantee the patient will benefit by participating in a particular trial; you may not even receive active medication. The obvious benefit to you is the special attention, close observation and a careful follow-up plan. All the details of your health care must be documented and frequently reviewed while participating in a research trial. Always know what you are getting into before becoming a research volunteer.

Being a research patient is much like being a 'test pilot' for the research industry. You 'fly' unexplored new treatments that must be tested before offered to the public at large. You help get the 'bugs' out of new drugs and devices. You expose yourself to the potential problems of untested treatments. You surrender yourself to the care of the research team. You inconvenience yourself to contribute to a better world!

Asking Questions And Getting Answers

Most people don't know how to respond when asked to participate in a research trial. Always find out why *you* are being asked to participate. Before agreeing to participate, make sure you read and clearly understand the consent form. Most of your questions will come from this document. Any questions you have must be answered before signing on. Don't be afraid to ask if the study is important original research or if is a routine 'must get done' type of trial required to reinforce data already collected. Although there are no guarantees, you should understand the potential benefits and risks. Be comfortable in asking *any* questions at *any* time throughout the duration of the trial. Remember; if you don't ask, you won't get any answers.

What about financial compensation? Does it exist? Of course it does. There has been an increased interest in reimbursing patients for out-of-pocket expenses incurred during these trials. Among those included are travel, parking and meals. Beyond this, subjects may be given financial incentives simply for their participation. This is especially so when patient recruitment is dependant upon advertising. Don't expect to make your fortune doing this and try not to let the money interfere with the basic principles of voluntary participation. Will your doctor be paid? Yes. His expenses will be reimbursed and he will likely receive payment for his professional time and activity. The amount of financial compensation to patient and doctor to a large extent depend upon the study sponsors. The Ethics Committee should ensure that the amount of money involved is not so excessive as to compromise patient recruitment or any other aspect of the trial.

Knowing Who's In Charge Besides You

The first thing a patient should ask is "Who's in charge?" This is particularly important if your physician/partner is not directly involved. Realize that research studies may be small and involve few patients or extremely large with many thousands of patients. A large group of professional research investigators (doctors) is required to conduct such studies. Typically there is a 'physician' in charge who is responsible for the conduct of the study at a specific site or location (e.g. office practice or hospital). There are study nurses or assistants who work closely with this investigator. At the higher level, there are study co-coordinators who visit the study sites to audit the conduct of the trial. There is also a principal investigator (usually at the head office of the study) who chairs a steering committee. There are a series of other committees to perform the many tasks required, e.g. Data Safety Monitoring Board that monitors the trial's progress, Publications committee, End-points committee, etc. All of this should be explained to you before you give your consent.

Informed Consent - What Are They Really Going To Do!

Every scientific research trial must have a consent form, which requires your signature before you participate. The consent form should include:

Components Of The Consent Form

- Background information
- Purpose and description of the study
- The potential risks (unforeseen as well) to the patient
- Potential benefits to the patient
- Person to contact if something happens or something goes wrong
- How the data is collected
- Details of who will see the data and other confidentiality issues
- Your rights as a participant
- What will happen upon completion of the study?
- What to expect if you drop out

Be sure to request a copy of the consent form for your health record. Remember, just as with any big decision you make, it is always a good idea to think about it for a few days before you agree to participate. Allow yourself time to fully understand what participation will mean to you and your family. You can withdraw from any study should you decide not to continue. Understand that the best time to decide not to participate is before you sign the consent form. An any other time your withdrawal creates statistical difficulties for the study. Discuss what will be required of you, time commitment, duration of the study, impact on your ability to travel, ability to take other medications, insurance concerns, etc. It is best for all concerned if you are informed before you consent. After all, this is why the form you sign is referred to as 'Informed Consent'.

Risks, Research Ethics And Good Practice Guidelines

It is fundamental to every research study to ensure patient safety at every level. Regardless, you must understand the possible complications or risks to you as a research subject. These must be clearly identified in the consent form. In general, the side effects are usually infrequent and not serious. However, some may be quite serious and cause you irreversible harm. The principal investigator should explain all of this to you in great detail. Although somewhat frightening at first, it is comforting to know that all research trials must be approved at a number of levels long before you are approached. The ethics review board (IRB) may be located at the local hospital or at a 'central ethics committee' location.

During the trial, your concerns about potential side effects and complications must be reported immediately. The investigator is legally bound to carefully record this information. Remember, that even patients taking the placebo (dummy) medication have side effects. These statistics are monitored periodically by the DSMB (Data Safety Monitoring Board) to ensure patient safety and the appropriateness of continuing the study. Your principal investigator is kept informed. Strategies exist to deal with issues which vary from study to study. In long-term studies the ethics committee must give annual approval for continuation.

The medical scientific establishment adheres to the principles established in what is termed 'Good Practice Guidelines' for conducting research on human subjects. To a large extent these guidelines are based on common sense and professionalism. They are a generally agreed upon code of ethical principles which are applied when using human beings as research subjects or 'test pilots'. All investigators and their assistants are expected to comply with these guidelines as laid out by organizations such as the World Medical Association and Medical Research Council of Canada. All investigators are expected to declare any conflicts of interest that may affect their participation in research activity. These codes are promoted by all hospitals and medical schools.

Knowing The Type Of Trial - Is This One For You?

Every research trial is designed to answer one or more specific questions. Trials vary in their complexity and scientific merit. In general they occur at various stages of development of the product being tested (the test drug, device or manoeuvre).

Trials Defined By Stage Of Development

Phase 1 – The first phase of a new drug or therapy is tested using animals and then humans. In general, 'normal' or healthy people are asked to volunteer for these trials. They are designed to address issues concerning safety of the intervention (Is it safe?). These require relatively small numbers of normal volunteers receiving the intervention.

Phase 2 – The second phase of testing addresses efficacy (Does it work?). Generally, these are designed to test if the drug is effective on patients who have the particular disease which the research team is investigating. This level of testing involves larger numbers of subjects with the disease receiving the intervention.

Phase 3 – The phase 3 trials are designed to measure exactly how well the particular drug or therapy works in practice (Does it work in the real world?). These require larger numbers of patients (thousands) who have the disease at various stages. These patients are then followed for longer periods of time on either the study intervention or a placebo (dummy drug).

Trials Defined By Structure Methodology

In *case control* trials, two patient populations are studied who receive (or have received) different treatments. Patients from each group are matched as closely as possible and outcome compared. In *crossover* trials, the subjects receive one intervention for a period of time and then change to a second intervention for another period of time. The patient's status during the two periods of time is compared. In a *placebo controlled* trial the active intervention is compared to an inactive intervention to see if the patient is being affected by the active intervention or the test conditions. Other studies may compare the results of two active interventions.

In *randomized* trials, patients are selected at random for inclusion in the various groups of the trial. This may be done with the investigators blinded or unblinded to the intervention each patient will receive. *Open label* studies are so-called because both patients and physicians know that the patient is receiving the actual intervention (active drug or therapy). In *blinded* studies (which can be quite complex), some portion of the process is unknown to patient or physician. *Double blind* trials imply neither patient nor physician is aware if the patient is receiving active or placebo intervention. Don't be too concerned, the steering committee knows what you are getting and in emergency situation, you can be identified. These studies are conducted to avoid bias; one example of which is to assume that side effects are due to the active drug when indeed it is due to the placebo.

In a drug study you may be taking active medication or placebo. That is why the pills you are taking are referred to as study drug and not referred to as the name of the particular drug being investigated. The structure and manoeuvres involved in research trials are designed to:

- Minimize bias
- Add statistical strength
- Ensure reproducibility
- Guarantee results can be generalized
- Maximize patient safety

Depending on the specific study and the randomization process, you may or may not know if you are receiving the active intervention. The investigator may not know either. Both can find out after the trial is completed, if you so choose. Each research trial has a different approach to how and when the study results are released. They also vary in the way they inform patients of the treatment they received during the trial. Most patients never find out but the information is accessible to you; all you have to do is ask!

Getting Advice And Informing Others; Don't Start Keeping Secrets

To be completely certain you are ready to participate in a research trial, take as much time as you need to think it through and get advice. Talk to people you trust. Find out important details such as any impact of participation on your insurance policy. Most consent forms will identify an alternate professional knowledgeable about the study but who is professionally uninvolved. They are specifically available to answer your questions from an unbiased perspective. The ethics committee could also serve this function. Just ask!

Always inform your family. They are your most important advocates and advisors. Always discuss your plan to participate with the professionals involved in your care. Priority Patients involve their personal physician in these decisions. Should you need to go to the emergency department for any reason, be sure to inform the nurses and doctors at the hospital that you are participating in a research trial and bring the study drug with you.

Thank You

It is critical that people volunteer to participate in research trials. Without you the progress of modern medicine would grind to a halt. Without new test pilots like you, there would be no new airplanes! Without voluntary participation of doctors and their patients many questions would remain unanswered and many diseases left untreated. Your participation is pivotal and no research can be conducted without *you*. While participation in a research trial is a serious matter, and should not be taken lightly, it is necessary if we hope to help others in the future to conquer illnesses such as cancer, diabetes and heart disease. Yes, you should pat yourself on the back for helping a great number of other people while at the same time helping to move medicine into the future.

Chapter Summary

- **Without you there would be no research!**

- **Read the consent form before you sign!**

- **The best time to say no is before you say yes (Don't start unless you plan to finish)!**

- **Understand the potential for problems.**

- **Know your commitment (number of visits, how long, etc.).**

- **Know their commitment (the research team).**

- **Know who's in charge.**

- **Know who to call when something is wrong.**

- **You may inconvenience yourself, BUT you make a significant contribution to a better world!**

Secrets About The Media

Patients are constantly exposed to the media and its coverage of scientific medical research. In fact, it is not uncommon for patients to get the results of scientific trials before doctors have time to assess this information. The media of course, is extremely hungry for 'late-breaking' news items. The medical establishment is extremely hungry for recognition of its successes and participation in scientific 'breakthroughs'. Even the research scientists themselves are hungry for such recognition which helps their funding and perhaps even feeds their ego. The media treatment of research creates medical 'rock stars' that regularly compete for the world's attention and their share of the limelight. The patient's interpretation of how the media reports these results heavily influences their reaction and subsequent expectations of the medical community. How should patients react? Are there guidelines available? Can or should patients be protected from media science? How do people do when science is exploited for the sake of sensationalism?

Where The Media's Interests Lie

It is not that the media does not care to report issues correctly and keep new research in perspective; it's simply a case of wanting to be the first to report. New and exciting information sells! Sensationalism is not unheard of in the media. Reporting unexciting results and failures of medical research just does not pay (except when it is noteworthy). This is why the media focuses on 'scientific' successes. This is frequently done prematurely and to a large extent incompletely. A new found drug widely reported as a potential cure for cancer, is later found to be merely a stepping stone in the treatment of a specific tumor. What is usually released are preliminary results which lack not only the details and limitations of the research, but also the alternative interpretations and analyses by those not committed to the success of the project. Patients are given high expectations perhaps only to later become disappointed and confused.

It is even difficult for some doctors to see through the sensationalism and manipulation of data. The best science reporter does not have the training necessary to critically appraise the results. In the excitement to bring forth new knowledge, the media in cooperation with the scientists and the funding agencies expose the public to early scientific results creating a demand for quick access to new treatments, the implications of which are largely unstated. Is this irresponsible or does the public have a right to hear early results? Considering that the new knowledge may have profound implications for the treatment of an individual patient, this process seems far too superficial. The patient becomes aware that a treatment exists but has no idea of its availability or appropriateness for their particular illness; a little knowledge becomes a dangerous thing.

Awareness and understanding are vastly different concepts!

So Who's Picking Up The Cheque?

If the media is reporting for sales and sensationalism, then what is the medical establishment getting out of the deal? Simple. They are generating identity and interest in their research, leverage with the public as well as the government, and most importantly, they are generating financial support. Public attention generated by media coverage encourages support from the government and granting agencies.

Good science garners support. Publicized science garners public interest! While the media is not necessarily a bad way to promote science, it has the potential for confusing or even misleading a large number of patients who are personally and emotionally attached to the issue. How can the general public be assured that what is presented is scientifically sound, reliable, complete, unbiased and applicable them as individuals. How can we tell how much of it is sensationalism? We can't. At least not from reading newspapers or watching the television. We must go to the source, read the published academic studies, and evaluate them the best we can. Only then can we be certain that we are getting the *relevant details* and not the *hype*. We are after all, paying the cheque. Shouldn't we get the whole truth?

Rock Stars And Research

Most scientists by nature are trustworthy, honest and credible individuals. Research can and should be done purely in the pursuit of new knowledge. Research supported and conducted by those primarily in pursuit of glory and fame (and market share) must be interpreted with an extra measure of criticism.

Medicine did not, until recently, have its own 'rock stars'. Doctors were conducting their own private research, gaining personal experience as they went along. They would pass their knowledge on to the next generation often by mentoring a younger physician. Although there were always 'well known' physicians, they were not made into the transient icons that are created by the media today!

After the appearance of television, the world of experimental research changed dramatically. Doctors were appearing on TV, in press conferences and documentaries. They were quick to gain celebrity status if they pioneered a new therapy. For example, if one looks back at the television appearances (news footage, etc.) of the first cardiovascular teams to attempt heart transplants, the race for not only the first heart transplant, but the race for exposure and celebrity status becomes immediately apparent. This is because, the bigger and better established the research team is, the easier it is for them to obtain funding for further research. Positive findings and research success are their goals.

That's Fantastic! - But What Does The Study Really Mean?

Can patients be taught how to interpret the media's reporting of scientific literature? It is not even easy to ensure that physicians understand the very complex results of large-scale clinical trials. Reporting by the media follows the usual process of clinical trial reporting in general.

Negative Test Results

Negative trials are rarely reported. Let's assume a new drug "B" is tested because it is felt to be better than the older drug "A". If the study finds that the old drug "A" is still better, the study will likely not be reported. It's not news! If the new drug "B" is equal to the old drug "A", the study may be reported but with far less enthusiastic fan fare. It is hard to develop a level of sensationalism, doesn't feed anyone's ego, and definitely doesn't translate into greater market share.

Positive Test Results

In the event that the new drug 'B' is better than 'A', Watch out! Drug 'B' will be reported as the latest, greatest, hottest breakthrough! This new drug will supposedly save more lives and should be used by *all* patients with the potential to benefit. Any doctor who does not prescribe it to their patients is considered poorly informed, old fashioned, behind the times, guilty of malpractice and definitely not practicing 'Evidence Based Medicine'. Drug 'B' will become the treatment of choice and generate large profits for the sponsoring corporation; greater market share.

Science - Reading The Results

There is no question that interpreting the results of scientific studies is beyond the ability of most patients and challenging to most physicians. What is *not* beyond the public's ability is to be cautious when observing the media coverage of "late breaking medical miracles". Do not assume you know the full story just because it is on TV, in the newspaper or on the six o'clock news. Do not assume the information is complete because it is being reported by credible journalists. Like everyone else, journalists must have the study results interpreted for them. The scientists themselves are the only source of original data but even then, it is subject to their personal interpretation! We have already seen the problems associated with interpretation and bias. In the past it took a long time for such results to translate into changes in clinical practice. Today, in part because of professional and media fanfare, clinical practice can change quickly, even before results have borne the test of time and critical analysis. As a patient, be careful not to insist on receiving a newly published treatment which you know little or nothing about. On the other hand, there is certainly nothing wrong with pursuing the matter in the medical literature rather than the media literature.

Media - Watch What You Watch!

Canada's government controlled public health system does not yet allow pharmaceutical companies to do 'direct consumer advertising'; directly advertising the benefits of certain drugs directly to the public. In the United States, this is a multimillion-dollar industry. Canadians will be exposed to this type of advertising in the many forms of American media presented to us. Be aware that this type of advertising is just that, not new scientific information! You are encouraged to consume a product that must be prescribed to you by a physician. You have to be careful to ensure that the treatment will benefit you as an individual not simply you as a medical problem.

Another interpretation of media reports on clinical trial results suggests a very clever and relatively cheap method of directly influencing many people (some patients, some not) without the expensive cost of formal advertising. It is well known how powerful the influence of media can be. It's unfortunate that great science is allowed to be cheapened by the way it is presented to the public. It's too bad that the impact of a truly fantastic new form of therapy is presented in such a way as to have many more people receive it than those patients who will actually gain significant benefit from it.

Perhaps we have just described the reason why most natural remedies, vitamins and supplements will never undergo rigorous scientific testing; the market for these products is already in the billions of dollars, based only on word of mouth and quasi-scientific literature. This is supported by a great deal of legal direct consumer advertising because natural remedies are not under the drug control offices of government.

Secrets Of Becoming An Educated Patient

Once you have decided to become a Priority Patient with all the attendant changes in your attitude and behaviour, I recommend you discuss your new health care action plan with your personal physician. Most doctors will be surprised by Priority Patients, but they will always respond favourably to an organized, informed patient. One of the most effective keys to becoming a Priority Patient is self-education. Lack of education promotes fear, anxiety, error and misunderstanding. Any disinterested patient who ignores their health care creates an added risk! The best and easiest way to start is to create or purchase your own personal health care diary.

What You Will Learn From Learning....

It has been said that the most important thing that students learn is how to learn. As an example, months after students have finished their studies they have forgotten a good percentage of what they learned throughout the school year. Hopefully, what they have not forgotten is how they studied, and how they acquired new knowledge. You see why it is so important to learn about your health care issues. Most people wait until they are in the midst of a health care crisis and then try to acquire knowledge under less than ideal circumstance. Those of you with established diseases should be continuously developing your skills at acquiring health information. An informed patient is not one who simply read an article in today's newspaper; they add that article to their growing library of information.

The best strategy is to read as much as you can about the health care issues that concern you and your family. You will find that it is not long before even the difficult medical terminology becomes easier to understand. Knowledge helps take the mystery out of medicine. You do not need to pursue a degree in anatomy or physiology to actively participate in your care.

We in the western world are convinced that medicine is based strictly on scientific fact. We tend to believe that since we are not scientists, we cannot possibly comprehend. This is a myth! Like anything else, if you make the effort to understand something, you become a better-educated consumer. With this attitude, you are on the path to becoming a Priority Patient! What you will discover is that medicine is not a pure science. It is based on science. In mathematics, 2+2=4. In medicine, decision-making is much more complex than a mathematical equation, with less predictable outcomes.

Medicine is the art of decision-making and the application of scientific knowledge to the individual patient.

Prepare Yourself, What You Will Find Is Quite Shocking!

Most patients believe that their physician is going to treat each patient in the same manner if they present with the same symptom. Let's hope not! As you begin to research your particular health concerns you will realize that doctors frequently disagree with each other and frequently debate the benefits of treatments. This is easily seen when one picks up a medical journal. Not only do patients have choices, but so do doctors when it comes to selecting treatment strategies.

In the media, we are confronted with sensational medical advances everyday. What is not revealed is the debate that arises amongst health care professionals (scientists) regarding new treatment approaches that have not yet been universally accepted. Once a treatment is proven and has survived the test of time it is generally adopted by all. New treatments may be advertised as applicable to everyone even though sufficient scientific evidence is lacking. Patients often misinterpret media releases as confirmed scientific fact and may even be critical of their physician for not using this fantastic new "cutting edge" therapy. The Priority Patient will actively participate by developing the necessary skills to critically appraise these media reports.

Doctors and other scientists conduct research attempting to prove that certain treatments are superior to others. They are not always right. The media seldom reports medical research failures. Indeed no one wants to report medical research failures. There appears to be no motivation for negative reporting. As health care consumers, we must do our own research not only for understanding, but for our own safety. You can limit treatment errors and misunderstandings by knowing more about what you are being asked to do. You should study as many of the opinions available when accepting a treatment strategy. Remember, the most important opinion will be the one that you and your doctor-partner have decided is best in your particular situation. Your personal physician's clinical experience with you allows insight, not supplied by the research paper. This is why for those important decision making times, it is advantageous to have a well-developed doctor/patient relationship.

The Priority Patient prepares in advance for these decision making discussions with any physician. There is more to doing your homework than saying to your doctor, "the guy on TV said there's a cure for AIDS but

I can't remember the name of it"! This superficial approach (you don't know what you're talking about) will not be appreciated. Asking your doctor "Would Nitrofurantoin be better than Sulfamethoxazole because of the bacteria's built up resistance?" will most definitely be met with surprise and profoundly raise the level of the discussion. Many patients may not make it to this point, but just asking for an explanation of the effect of the two antibiotics has a positive effect. Even if your question is flawed, you will have gained new knowledge from asking it (not to mention an added level of respect!).

Participation 101

You may be asking yourself "how exactly does becoming educated help me to become a Priority Patient?". It's simple. If you are educating yourself about your health, your level of interest quickly translates into involvement and participation and more self-confidence. Participation in your own health care means sharing responsibility for the decisions that are being made and feeling confident about the choices you have made.

Involvement requires education upon which you can base your actions. Participation increases your ability to make the right decisions. This new ability will boost your confidence. In turn you make yourself a priority. If you believe you are a priority, others will believe so too. You have no idea how much this step separates you from most people who don't seem to care!

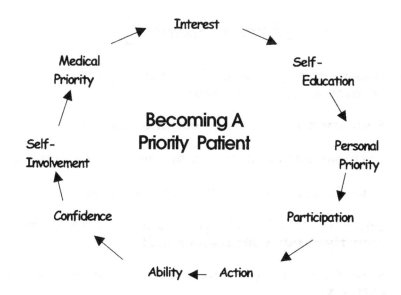

There is much to be gained by participating in all aspects of your individual health care.

What You Gain From Participation

- A raised level of communication
- Better appreciation of outcomes
- Respect
- Improved ability to live with chronic illness
- A better appreciation of medical media sensationalism
- A better definition of your role and responsibilities
- An awareness of the choices
- A more personalized approach to your health care

The Priority Patient has no difficulty assisting the health care team by offering a personal perspective to the medical problem. The Priority Patient will also factor in the human side of their health care needs and will no longer be treated as just a 'symptom' or 'disease'. You will become a person with individual complaints and individual circumstances. You are a Priority!

For those who encounter medical professionals who do not appreciate an educated patient, keep in mind that it is your health. The Priority Patient will make every attempt to continue and improve the doctor/patient *partnership* by: 1) actively accepting responsibility for *shared* decisions and, 2) carefully following the chosen treatment recommendations. You are the only one who has to live with the decisions that are made. So take responsibility and take charge!

Chapter Summary

- **Inform your personal physician of your plan to become a Priority Patient.**

- **Education is the key to communication.**

- **Both patients and physicians must earn respect!**

- ***Your* illness requires *your* involvement!**

- **Don't be afraid to ask questions – it's not only your right but your responsibility!**

- **Most doctors appreciate a patient that participates actively!**

- **Get a medical dictionary! Look things up!**

- **Read, Read, Read and Read some more!**

Keys To Discovering Medical Information
Part A - Traditional Sources

There are so many sources offering medical information it can be very confusing. Much of the information is excellent, some of it isn't. Acquiring information is most important. The specific sources you use will vary from time to time depending on your need and preferences. Try to experience all of the sources. The more informed you become, the more you build on your Priority position. Traditional sources of information include:

- Doctor
- Nurse
- Walk-in clinics
- Health Units
- Government Offices
- Book stores
- Alternative medical practitioners

- Nurse Practitioner
- Pharmacist
- Hospitals
- Library
- Medical Associations
- Pamphlets
- Magazines

Sometimes the personal physician can be the best starting point. They may clarify issues for you in advance, making it easier to narrow down your search for the information required. Professionals in general are good primary sources of information and can put you on to other sources.

When you do locate the information of interest, consider extending your search to the references supplied to support what you have read. References are the original 'links' that we now have on Internet sites today. They often lead to a wealth of information that you would otherwise not discover. Use multiple sources (audio, visual, etc.). Don't be concerned if some authors disagree. The more disagreement you uncover, the more likely it is that there is no single answer to your question. The topic may be under active debate and you can learn a lot by getting the different perspectives. Keep your medical dictionary close at hand. Be aware and don't be afraid to dig deep!

Before You Begin...Take A Research Crash Course!

It may seem overwhelming when you begin to conduct research into your particular medical problem. You may or may not have a research background. Relax; this process is no different than what you did for a school/office project or assignment, it's only the subject and the language that's changed. That's why you have a dictionary! You may feel that you are not in the position to decide what is or is not credible, however you will get much better at judging the quality of information with experience. Here are a few starter points:

Beginner's Hints

- Talk to your doctor first (they may provide the information you are looking for or at least point you in the right direction).
- Know the *exact* name of the condition you are investigating (medicine has many like-sounding terms e.g. Pemphagus, Pemphagoid).
- Call national or international associations/societies (e.g. Alzheimer's).
- Read popular magazine articles (e.g. Chatelaine, Reader's Digest).
- Speak to your pharmacist and check local pharmacies for information pamphlets.
- Look up relevant terms in the encyclopedia and dictionary (purchase a medical dictionary).
- Check your local library (health and disease section).
- If you have access, visit a university library (bring money for photocopies if you do not have borrowing privileges).
- Find a good summary review of the topic in general before you get too specific.
- References are an excellent source of further information.

Once you think you have obtained enough information (we suggest that this means you have consulted at least 5 *different* sources), digest it and summarize it for yourself. Only then consider presenting your findings and list of ongoing concerns to your personal physician. The next meeting with your physician will be more meaningful. You have now done a great deal to improve the level of communication with your physician/partner. Your physician has the clinical experience to clarify any misconceptions and match the newly acquired information to your specific problem and personal circumstance. He may now direct you to his own medical literature for more sophisticated and current perspectives. Do you see how valuable a good doctor/patient relationship is? This simply can't occur in a walk-in clinic or emergency department!

Professional Medical Literature, Watch Out!!!

The most important problem in turning to the professional medical literature is that you do not have the proper training to assess it. Even those who are trained do not always properly assess the literature. There are resources available to teach you how to critically assess medical information. Many websites exist to help patients and doctors understand how to critically evaluate a journal article. Be aware, there are currently over 20,000 medical journals published annually. Even the best medical journals occasionally publish bad studies. For this reason, in 1997 the British Medical Journal published a series of guides to assist the general public in evaluating and understanding the medical literature. These guides are accessible online at www.bmj.com and can be found at any library that carries the BMJ:

British Medical Journal: Guides For Evaluating Medical Literature

- The Medline database, *BMJ* 1997;315:180-183 (19 July)

- Getting your bearings (deciding what the paper is about) *BMJ* 1997; 315:243-246 (26 July)

- Assessing the methodological quality of published papers *BMJ* 1997;315 (2 August)

- Statistics for the non-statistician. I: Different types of data need different statistical tests *BMJ* 1997;315:364-366 (9 August)

- Statistics for the non-statistician. II: "Significant" relations and their pitfalls *BMJ* 1997;315:422-425 (16 Aug)

- Papers that report drug trials *BMJ* 1997;315:480-483 (23 August)

- Papers that report diagnostic or screening tests *BMJ* 1997;315:540-543 (30 August)

- Papers that tell you what things cost (economic analyses) *BMJ* 1997;315:596-599 (6 Sept)

- Papers that summarize other papers (systematic reviews and meta-analyses) *BMJ* 1997; 315:672-675

- Papers that go beyond numbers (qualitative research) *BMJ* 1997;315:740-743 (20 September)

There are many more guides on the internet (some of which are even disease specific) to help you learn the art of assessing the validity and relevance of medical information.

The Doctor/Patient Relationship Is Important To Your Personal Research

There are many ways to critically assess medical information. Your doctor has already been trained to do this (hopefully, he does it well). When you begin to read medical journals and published information, you will find it difficult to understand the more complex issues of statistical analysis. This is when your physician will come in handy. Your physician may question the usefulness of one or two of your sources because of some of the following problems:

Reasons Your Doctor May Disagree With A Study

- Your specific problem was not the focus of the study.
- Different patients were selected in the study (e.g. different gender, age).
- Not enough patients were studied.
- The study was not 'blinded' (potential for bias).
- The study was too short.
- The effects were not significant enough for your circumstances.
- The data analysis contained error.
- The results may not be applicable to your situation.
- The results were significant for a large patient population but the effects on any individual are totally unknown.

When you find something that interests you, read it thoroughly, attempt to understand it, critically assess it (to your best ability), and then formulate questions to ask your doctor regarding the proposed treatment. Your doctor will be much more likely to respond positively if you come in prepared. Try to bring in a photocopy of the article for your doctor in case he needs more time to review it. Do not simply arrive, hand your doctor a study and expect a detailed explanation. Like you, he needs time to digest and critically appraise. If possible, send your doctor the article in advance or ask to discuss it during a follow-up appointment.

Once again, this type of exchange *cannot* occur in a walk-in clinic or emergency department environment. A mature doctor/patient partnership is built on a foundation of trust, understanding and the sharing of knowledge and responsibility. The Priority Patient continues to grow and expand his knowledge of health care issues pertaining to their individual situation. They use this knowledge to continuously improve their health and health care by sharing the complex decision making process with a physician who knows them as a unique individual in the setting of mutual respect.

Chapter Summary

- ᴏ⊸ **The more you develop your research skills and critical thinking the better they get!**

- ᴏ⊸ **The Internet is a valuable resource...if you don't already know how to use it – LEARN!**

- ᴏ⊸ **Don't believe everything you read simply because it is in print!**

- ᴏ⊸ **Recognize that there are many sources of medical information.**

- ᴏ⊸ **Don't misinterpret your physician's negativity for ignorance (their clinical experience often outweighs the latest breaking clinical trial results)!**

- ᴏ⊸ **Establish trust and respect with your doctor!**

- ᴏ⊸ **If you have to be sick "BE SMART"!**

www.lots_a_luck/canuck.ca

"Internet can be a great ally for public health. It can help empower patients, it can help citizens make healthy lifestyle choices...The key is to find ways for the valid, the relevant, the helpful online information to be distinguished from the unreliable or downright bogus"

David Byrne - European commissioner
for health and consumer protection
The Medical Post · December, 2002

Keys To Discovering Medical Information
Part B - Surviving The Internet

Increasingly as people become comfortable with the Internet, they are turning to the World Wide Web for medical information and advice. Beware, unlike the professional medical literature, there are no controls on the content to which you are exposed. There is much misinformation out there! You have to be careful. The volume of health care information available on the Internet is awesome. The amount of scientific information available on any medical problem is infinite and continuously growing. It is both fortunate and problematic that patients have such unlimited access to information that may well be beyond their ability to comprehend. Even if they do understand the concepts and terminology, they may not be able to apply the information to their particular medical condition. For example, you understand what a particular treatment can accomplish without knowing whether it is suitable for you. Is a coronary bypass operation the best treatment for every patient with angina? NO. Remember the wisdom of medicine is the ability to apply scientific knowledge to the individual patient. You can't get those years of training and experience from the net!

Without the proper skills to assess the credibility of a particular website, patients can find information about their personal health issue; information they are unable to verify. Asking 'Joe from Idaho' about your angina on the health chat network may be misleading and even dangerous. You would be better to start with the American Heart Association website. This is not to say that health chat networks are not well suited for personal discussions regarding your illness. It simply means that you must be cautious in interpreting the information you obtain from this source. You would not ask the grocery clerk down the street about your test results or the lump on your neck, so why trust a perfect stranger over the Internet?

The Internet has unlimited potential to spread medical knowledge worldwide. Until now, the ability of people around the world to obtain medical knowledge has been limited to local library research. The Internet offers unparalleled access to medical knowledge, fantastic yet frightening!

Knock Knock ...Who's There?

In this chapter we are assuming that you know how to surf the net. That does not in any way imply that you know how to assess who you are dealing with when you log on. We suggest you start by looking at the 'URL address' in your web browser's 'address' line, at the top of the page. For example, you are reading information about a revolutionary new drug on the market that is "guaranteed to cure your green spots". If the URL address is from a reputable institution like Stanford University in California (http://www.med.stanford.edu/MedCenter/green-spots) then you can probably trust the content of the website. If by chance, the URL shows a *personal* website (http://www.angelfire/homepages/ Bob'smedicalpages/green-spots/html) don't automatically trust the content. Whenever possible, verify the information with a well-known, credible medical website.

Some websites will actually have names of doctors on them such as "Dr. Joe's Medical Web". While some be may be licensed physicians and offer valid information, others may not. Anyone, anywhere in the world can post a website. It is important that you realize you have no way of verifying the credentials of these individuals. You do not know them. They can claim to have any university degree, research experience or hospital appointment. How would you know the difference? You don't. Beware. Some specific URL address information is easily identifiable. Learn the codes. Here is what you need to know when looking at a URL address:

Identifying URL Abbreviations (examples)

gov. – This abbreviation stands for government. Always a reliable source of information.

edu. – This stands for university or college. It is an educational institution. A terrific source for medical information!

org. – This one is tricky! It stands for organization. It does not necessarily ensure that they are a reputable organization. You should research the name of the organization further.

assn.- This abbreviation is for association. Again follow these links with caution. There are many associations that have few or no credentials (for example there is a "kill the purple dinosaur association") On the contrary there are many professional associations with excellent credentials (e.g. "Canadian Medical Association"). Do your homework!

Concentrate your search efforts on professional organizations, hospitals, recognized universities and government departments familiar to you. Some *apparent* educational institutions online may be formed by individuals and self-proclaimed experts. Again, beware. Use sites that you have heard of before such as Stanford University, Harvard University, McGill University or the University of Toronto. A real university should exist in a place other than cyber space. Pure cyber institutions can be created by anyone!

Journals, Journals And More Journals

If you really want first hand medical information online, you can search the medical literature. Yes you can! There are excellent online sources listing published academic journals. All major professional medical journals are online. Some offer *temporary, trial* or even *permanent* subscriptions at a price. There are many excellent *free* sources. For example, you can search journals such as the British Medical Journal, The New England Journal of Medicine, The Journal of the American Medical Association, and many more. For the advanced Priority Patient the information available is truly limitless. There are even websites that will search out the information you are interested in and email it to you on a regular basis. Try http://www.amedeo.com/ for this type of service. Online medical literature should never replace the advice of your personal physician!

Medical Journal Resources

Free medical journals online: http://www.freemedicaljournals.com/

Highwire Press – Stanford University free journal listing: http://highwire.stanford.edu/lists/freeart.dtl

Journal of the American Medical Association - (JAMA): http://jama.ama-assn.org/issues/current/toc.html

The British Medical Journal (BMJ): http://bmj.com

The New England Journal of Medicine (NEJM): http://www.nejm.org/

Stanford University's research tool for doctors: http://www.skolar.com/

★ ★ ★ ★ ★

"Australians get [government sponsored] online access to health-care reviews"

Graham Worrall
The Medical Post · December, 2002

Guidelines And Other Professional Resources

In addition to all of the available medical information provided by journals, patients can access many guidelines and resources listed by reputable institutions. Even if people are uncomfortable reading medical research (the jargon can sometimes be quite confusing!), there are good patient information websites and a number of nontechnical, user-friendly, websites devoted to informing the public about good practice guidelines and other health issues. Some very informative sites can be found on the Internet. Many of them are listed at the following resource websites:

Information Websites And Guidelines

World Health Organization: http://www.who.org/.

Canadian Medical Association (CMA): http://www.cma.caHealthContent/ASP/Index.asp.

American Medical Association (AMA): http://www.ama-assn.org/ama/pub/category/3158.html.

Harvard guide to online resources http://countweb.med.harvard.edu/web_resources/med/.

Disease Control and Prevention: http://www.cdc.gov/.

Agency for Health Care Research and Quality: links that help patients choose wisely: http://www.ahcpr.gov/consumer/.

There are also an infinite number of libraries that can be accessed online! Almost every medical university is online and offers web access to their catalogues. Here is a listing of some libraries that offer a searchable catalogue:

Libraries Online

Exeter Medical Library: http://www.ex.ac.uk/library/eml/hotlinks.html.

Health Sciences Library: http://www-medlib.med.utah.edu/.

Countway Library of Medicine (Harvard): http://countweb.med.harvard.edu/web_resources/med/.

U.S. National Library of Medicine: http://www.nlm.nih.gov/.

WWW Virtual Library: Biosciences: Medicine: http://www.ohsu.edu/cliniweb/wwwvl/.

There are also medical encyclopedias and dictionaries online. They come in as many as nine or more languages! This is not a bad place to start for the junior reader and the uninitiated.

Dictionaries And Encyclopedias

Glossary of Technical and Popular Medical Terms in Nine European Languages: http://allserv.rug.ac.be/~rvdstich/eugloss/welcome.html.

Medlineplus Medical Encyclopedia: http://www.nlm.nih.gov/medlineplus/encyclopedia.html.

Merck Home Edition: http://www.merckhomeedition.com/.

For The Brave Amongst You...

In addition to institutions, journals, guidelines, resource lists, libraries, etc. there are literally millions of websites dedicated to medical topics. If you feel that you are able to discern between fact and fiction, there are also an infinite number of search engines that will help you explore the virtual medical world!

Search Engines

Pubmed: http://www.pubmed.com.

Medical Matrix: http://www.medmatrix.org.

Medscape: http://www.medscape.com/.

Martindale's Health Science Guide: http://www-sci.lib.uci.edu/HSG/MedicalCardio.html.

MedicineNet: http://www.medicinenet.com/Script/Main/hp.asp.

Praxis MD Best Practice of Medicine: http://praxis.md/bpm.

Dogpile (a meta search engine)**:** http://www.dogpile.com.

There are also a variety of websites dedicated to the health issues that concern certain groups of individuals or general health knowledge. For example:

Women's health : http://www.womens-health.com/
Men's issues: http://www.vix.com/pub/men/health/health.html
Child health: http://www.crha-health.ab.ca/hlthconn/topics/child.htm
Senior's health: http://www.thecareguide.comindex.php?viewpage=home
&viewsection=resources&department =Health+and+Wellness&id=274

A large variety of websites are dedicated to specific diseases and illnesses. If you plan to search the web for a particular condition, try typing it in the address bar. You will begin with www. then the name of the disease (e.g. cancer), and then end it with .ca if you are interested in a Canadian website or .com if you want an international (mostly American) website. Your address should look like this: www.cancer.ca . In most cases this works quite well and will take you to a society like the Canadian Cancer Society.

Another excellent source for website addresses and information are popular magazines and television websites. Publications such as Reader's Digest (www.rd.com), Chatelaine (www.chatelaine.com) and Prevention (www.prevention.com), all have excellent websites with health links. Many television shows that discuss health topics such as Oprah Winfrey (www.oprah.com) and Komo4's Healthwatch (www.komotv.com/healthwatch/) also have health information and references.

It is impossible to control the quality of the content you encounter. By the way, the author of this book can take no responsibility for what individual websites may contain. In mature doctor/patient relationships, the patient's new found knowledge and understanding will elevate the level of communication with her physician partner. The decision-making process regarding individual patients will benefit by fine-tuning the application of collective knowledge. Remember, it is your doctor's responsibility to help you clarify *your* interpretation of *your* problems; it is *your* condition and you are the one who needs to understand it!

Cyber-pharmacies

Yes, you can purchase your medications cheaper online. This is a relatively new phenomenon. However, if you plan to have your medical prescriptions filled by an online pharmacy, do the best you can to ensure that the product you receive is indeed what you ordered. What you miss in this process is interaction with and advice from a pharmacist. The pharmacist does not know you personally and cannot make you aware of concerns he has about you taking certain medication. The cyber-pharmacist cannot personally advise you about drug interactions. In your particular case, it may not be worth the savings to lose the personal touch. In other situations (long-term, stable-dose medications) it may not matter. The same advice applies to alternative remedies.

Alternative Health Care Online

If you are searching for information regarding alternative medicine such as homeopathy, acupuncture, herbalism, Ayurveda, etc., there are websites with valuable information. However, always advise your physician of any additional treatments you are currently taking or considering, to ensure compatibility with your prescription medication. These might include vitamins, herbs, seeds, etc. Many physicians are quite accepting of alternative therapies as long as they do not interfere with your other medications or are perceived as dangerous to your health. There are a number of respected alternative medical traditions that may be integrated with your current health care plan. Once again, Buyer Beware! Do not use herbs, etc. with the assumption that they will not hurt you! Some herbal remedies can have negative effects when mixed with prescription medications. Always reveal to your doctor any herbal (or other) remedies you are taking before he writes you a prescription!

There are a number of respectable websites that discuss alternative treatment therapies. You should be as critical here as you are with the professional and non-professional medical websites that you are using. Be aware that alternative therapies at this time are not governed by the Canadian Federal Drug Administration.

Alternative Websites

Holistic Online : A website dedicated to holistic healing. http:www.holistic -online.com.

Dr.Weil : Dr. Weil is a long-standing advocate and expert on Health and wellness. A wealth of general health information. http://www.drweil.com/.

Whole Health Med (Healing Paths) : A website developed by doctors that contains alternative treatment options as well as conventional options for conditions such as carpal tunnel syndrome and kidney stones. Good drug, supplement and therapy reference library.http:/www.wholehealthmd.com/

Alternative Medicine Channel : The alternative medicine channel is full of information regarding alternative treatment options. Includes naturopathy and Chinese medicine. http:/www.alternativemedicinechannel.com/.

Alternative medicine websites are loaded with nutrition information. Even if you are not interested in pursuing alternative remedies, you may want to visit these sites to gather nutritional advice.

Watching Out For Scams!

There are some really bad websites giving bad information. It is often difficult for the novice to recognize these sites. Because of this, several sites were created which are dedicated to uncovering health fraud on the Internet. One of the biggest sites dedicated to sharing information about bad websites is Quackwatch. Their website is located at: http://www.quackwatch.com/. While some of these 'quackery' or health fraud websites are extremely useful, they too can be created by just about anyone. Read with care!

Chapter Summary

- **Medical chat websites are just *chat*!**

- **Recognize the difference between professional and non-professional websites.**

- **Media websites are Media!**

- **Understand the implications of ordering prescriptions and remedies online.**

- **All information gained from websites requires critical analysis and careful interpretation!**

- **Beware of giving personal information to any website.**

- **Make your doctor aware of all online advice you plan to follow (including home remedies).**

- **All research is good research when conducted from a critical perspective.**

Secrets Of Surviving A Teaching Hospital

I am a former associate professor of medicine at the University of Toronto. Universities with medical schools require close affiliations with one or more hospitals. The main purpose of this affiliation or partnership is the education of young medical professionals. Another component of this relationship is research. Both education and research require a large number of patients to satisfy the needs of hundreds of medical students to be exposed to thousands of patients; people with diseases. These hospitals have a special commitment to education and research. It is not unusual for them to have several types of students with several levels of seniority.

Teaching Hospitals - Care vs. Education

If you have ever been admitted to an academic teaching hospital you will be quite familiar with the content of this chapter. The health care establishment consists of a large number of distinct professional groups, nurses, physicians, surgeons, psychiatrists, midwives, dentists, laboratory technologists, etc. Each of these professional groups has developed thorough, in-depth and progressive educational programs to help their students acquire the necessary knowledge and skills needed in their chosen profession. Some of these teaching programs are attached to colleges or large universities. The teachers are professionals who have both an academic appointment at the university and a clinical appointment at the hospital. It is routine for patients in these hospitals to be asked to participate in the teaching process perhaps even more than once! Some educational facilities are private, stand alone institutions. All of these students require exposure to a variety of patients in a clinical setting in order to gain the experience necessary to complete the practical segment of their education.

Medical and nursing students have perhaps the most intimate exposure to patients who are hospitalized for investigation and treatment of disease. Other educational settings offering contact with patients are, laboratories, doctors' offices, clinics, etc. Wherever student/patient contact is made it is very important that the teacher, the student and the patient have a complete understanding of why the student is there and what the student's role is as a member of the health care team. All too often the student is inflicted upon the patient without a clear explanation of the purpose for their presence.

The Patient - Nothing's Possible Without You!

Yes, you are perfectly within your rights to refuse to be exposed to students of any kind. No, this will not compromise your care. Given the right set of circumstances, you can gain a great deal by participating in the education of these junior members of the health care team. You will not receive compensation for helping students to learn, but there are other benefits. For example, they have the time to get details of your medical history that could otherwise be overlooked. When they present their findings to their teacher, you stand to learn much more about your condition and your care. Frequently these issues are presented and debated in your presence. You are the key to all meaningful education in the health sciences. Your complaints, problems, symptoms and diseases are the 'Big Bang' of the education process! Health care education is totally dependant on the cooperation of volunteer patients.

Although rarely appreciated, the patient is the real teacher! You teach by allowing the student to verbally and physically explore you. Only you demonstrate the uniqueness of each patient. You are the only one who can personalize a symptom or disease. You and the student discuss and hopefully realize that it is not just a symptom or a disease, it is a real life *person* with a problem. There is a great mutual trust created by the student's examination and the patient's willing participation. Your contribution consists of revealing private medical information as well as exposing your physical self, all in the name of education. Not infrequently this is done in a setting in which both the student and patient may feel insecure and vulnerable. These emotions fade with time as students progress and patients become comfortable with the process. No matter how comfortable the two parties become, it should not be forgotten that this is an important yet delicate process. Students should never forget that this is a very personal encounter not to be taken for granted. Patients must always appreciate their pivotal role as a teaching subject. The student's real education culminates with the realization that the treatment of disease is in reality the treatment of ordinary people who have diseases.

Before you agree to participate in the teaching process, get a number of things clear with the supervising teacher and with the student as well. Remember the intimacy of this process. Don't blindly enter into this exchange without first defining it for yourself. Make sure they know how you feel and what your expectations are! To avoid uncomfortable experiences with teachers and students, the patient must have a clear understanding of the following:

- The student's needs
- The teacher's plan and role
- The patient's rights and role
- The education process

If admitted to a teaching hospital, expect to be asked to participate and do so at the level with which you are comfortable.

The Student - Watch Them Grow!

Students come in different shapes and sizes. Remember they are people like you who have chosen a career in the health sciences. They have individual personalities. They have character and dignity. They may be shy, silly, confident, arrogant, etc. They have a duty to you and the most important part of that duty is to ensure your comfort and safety and confidentiality!

Students also come to you at different levels of their training. First year students are usually young, naive, shy, frightened, etc. Final year students are more likely confident, empathetic, etc. During their years of learning they are given increasing levels of responsibility. For you that implies they take increasing levels of responsibility for your care. More is expected of them. Just as a mechanic's apprentice near the end of his training should be able to diagnose and repair the problem with limited supervision, so too should the student doctor or nurse.

As they grow and mature in their years of training, students are exposed to more complex patients and problems. However, until they formally become a certified practitioner of their chosen field, they are always responsible to their superiors who should always have the patient's best interests in mind. The student should present:

- Photo I.D.
- Appropriate dress
- Identity of school and program
- Initial introduction (supervisor with student)
- Confirmation of identity at each subsequent encounter
- Explanation of their actions
- A summary of their findings

Most student/patient encounters will occur at the patient's bedside if in hospital. However, patients may also be asked to participate in group learning by students. These encounters may occur in lecture theaters, clinic rooms or in hospitals. Several students may be involved either as a group or one after the other. The patient should feel free to limit the number of students at any one time.

The Teacher/Supervisor - Ultimately Responsible

Initially at least, the supervisor must speak with you before you are exposed to any student. You must be made aware of the number of students who will be directly involved in your care. You should also know when and how often they will be with you. You will also want to know what they are allowed to do and what their supervisors expect them to do. It is always nice to know how long they plan to work with you. You should be advised by the supervisor in advance if you are expected to participate in the student's evaluation. DO NOT deal with a student unless you have met the instructor and have been formally introduced.

The instructor is responsible for building the relationship between you and the education process. If you are approached by a teacher who requests your participation, there is a minimum amount of information you will require in order to decide if you will volunteer.

- Name and title of instructor
- Academic/clinical appointment and institution
- Years of teaching experience
- The student's limitations
- The student's level of experience
- The confidentiality of the process
- What is expected of the patient
- What is expected of the student

You might ask for a printed set of goals so that you can assist with the education process. Ask that you be allowed to comment on the student's performance.

The Medical School Is For Patients Too!

Priority Patients can put themselves through their own 'medical school for patients'. Become a student yourself! The tuition is affordable, the resources are unlimited, the benefits are awesome! In your early years you teach yourself how to pursue a healthy lifestyle designed to prevent premature disease. You will learn the importance of regular exercise, a balanced diet, and you will learn how to avoid unhealthy habits such as cigarette smoking. As you progress, you may become exposed to diseases that require your greater attention. You may become diabetic. You then learn how to cope with your disease. You actively pursue knowledge and become aware of potential problems and treatment options. Your education will help you build experience and you will learn to value a strong and continuous doctor/patient partnership. You will also make yourself aware of the complexities of the health care universe: medical trends, changing practice patterns and attitudes, fragmentation and funding of health care. As you navigate this universe, you will learn the importance of personal health care record-keeping, active participation in your care and the importance of sharing the responsibility of decision-making with your physician/partners.

Introduction To Safety And You: You're In Charge!

Why consider for even a moment that we could be in danger while interacting with the medical establishment. Tragically we are. In fact, in a study initiated by the Robert Wood Johnson Foundation in March of 2001, 95% of physicians reported that they had witnessed a "serious" medical error. The current medical universe has no accurate accounting mechanism for such problems. In the past, and even now, errors are unrecognized, denied by those who commit them, covered up and hence significantly under reported. The causes of many incidents remain unexplored and uncorrected. Despite our best efforts, serious action is seldom taken to ensure the safety of future patients. There is a movement developing among medical professional societies which encourages physicians to:

- Make all efforts to minimize complications.
- Disclose this early to patient and family.
- Admit when an error has occurred.
- Actively pursue policies designed to prevent recurrence.

Taking Care Of Yourself

The primary focus of every individual should be on preventive practices. If you take care of your health you will use the health care system less. Each and every time you interact with the health care universe you are potentially at risk! For example, in a Canadian hospital in 1996, a 33-year-old man died when he was accidentally injected with potassium chloride (the chemical used as a lethal injection to execute death row prisoners in the United States). He was admitted for a routine kidney infection. The wrong medication was administered. When the patient protested, he was told that it was the doctor's orders. This is truly a tragic and preventable horror story.

Similar accidents occurs approximately 10,000 times a year in Canadian hospitals; patients are given the wrong medication or the wrong dose. This is the number of *reported* fatal incidents. Worse yet, patients who are given the wrong medication and survive, are not included in this estimate! This point illustrates how important it is for patients to be aware of the details of their treatment.

Taking The First Steps Toward Safer Health Care

The first step to take is to ensure that your personal physician is aware of everything that is happening. He is your partner in this health care business. If you don't have a partner/physician, assume you are a total stranger to any and all medical professionals you encounter. The best and most effective strategies for keeping yourself safe are:

Taking Charge

- Assume you are a stranger and identify yourself at every encounter.
- Be informed - know your illnesses and your options.
- Keep accurate and up to date health records - keep a personal health diary.
- Coordinate your health care team - keep everyone informed.
- Ask questions, and discuss your concerns before proceeding.
- Have personal support - get family members involved in the process.
- Follow your doctor's advice - work together to solve your problems.
- Maintain a healthy dose of skepticism!
- Don't let things happen if you aren't sure they should happen.

For those of you who want to stay informed, visit patient safety websites such as the National Patient Safety Foundation's website at www.npsf.org. Remember Murphey's Law, "If anything can go wrong, it will", it's only a matter of time.

Safety Tools And Safety Rules

Many sections of this book cover issues regarding patient safety. In fact the majority of the book addresses safety issues in one manner or other. This section will summarize the more important tools and rules that you can use to stay alert and stay safe. Remember if it can happen it will!

Prescription Safety

- Always ask if the prescription is necessary.
- Have the prescription explained in terms of how it works and why you need it.
- Ask the doctor for the correct dosage and write it down (in case the pharmacist does not read the doctor's writing correctly).
- Notify your doctor immediately of any side effects.
- Always read your prescription label to ensure that it matches your name.

- Request an explanation of how the prescription works from the pharmacist.
- Never take a medication to which you have previously had a reaction.
- Never accept medication in hospital, <u>especially intravenously</u> (in your vein or I.V.) without having the nurse re-check the dosage and name of the prescription twice against your chart and identification wristband.
- Ask if there is any interaction with your other medications.

Hospital Safety

- Always identify yourself to everyone you encounter.
- Make certain your wristband and chart are checked every time a test is performed or medication is administered.
- Make sure everyone who touches you is wearing a fresh pair of gloves!
- Request an explanation for everything!
- Try to avoid being left alone in the hospital (have a family member stay with you - and never leave a child unattended in hospital!).
- Watch that basic rules of cleanliness are observed (medical personnel wash their hands each time they enter your room to work with you, if a needle is dropped that it is discarded and a fresh one used and that equipment is washed or wiped before it is used on you).
- Inform someone immediately if you see blood, etc. on the floor, bed or facilities!
- Question the health care worker if you do not feel comfortable with something they are doing to you or your family member.
- Do not allow yourself to be intimidated! Make yourself heard and understood!
- Tell someone if you see hair on your sheets.
- Record the name of every health care worker with whom you are in contact during your stay.

Safety In The Doctor's Office

- Ensure you lie down on a fresh piece of paper on the examining room table.
- If you are requested to remove your clothes, you should be supplied a cover-up (hospital gown, sheet, etc.).
- Tell your doctor if something he is doing is making you uncomfortable.
- If you like your doctor but their office is unclean, do not be afraid to politely mention it to the support staff (i.e. the secretary or nurse). If you are afraid to offend them, you could always anonymously send them a bottle of cleaning fluid in the mail with a short note!
- Request that a nurse be present for all examinations of a private nature.
- Remember, the physical examination should be appropriate for the problem you have described (a sprained ankle does not require a breast examination)!

- Don't be embarrassed to ask the purpose of all aspects of the physical examination.
- Minors should be accompanied by an adult.
- If your doctor cannot answer your questions, request a second opinion.
- Note whether or not your doctor writes a prescription for every complaint.
- Make sure your doctor writes their prescriptions clearly so that they will not be misinterpreted by the pharmacist.
- Remember you could be the 1 in 500 (who suffers a bad outcome), so think about saying "NO" and consider the consequences of your treatment options thoroughly.

The Red Flags Are Raised, What Should You Do?

Many patients are too intimidated to react when something appears to be wrong. This may be one of the reasons that so many tragedies occur with medical errors. On occasion, patients have even had an unnecessary operation because they were mistaken for someone else! This is a most easily preventable error. If you feel that something wrong is about to happen, STOP IT! If you feel that something wrong has happened, REPORT IT IMMEDIATELY! For example, if a doctor is sending you for a test that does not seem correct (e.g. they are sending you for a pelvic x-ray and you have a lung condition) stop them immediately and request an explanation. The same holds true if you suspect that someone has inappropriately touched you or your child. DO NOT WAIT, question them immediately. If you do not get an adequate explanation for the event or misunderstanding, there are steps that you should take.

What Should You Do?

- Confront the offending individual.
- Request a thorough explanation.
- Discuss with the individual's supervisor (if it is a nurse – the Charge Nurse, if it is a doctor – speak to the Chief of Staff).
- Document the event early and be thorough.
- Ask for a chart review.
- Speak to the patient advocate (realize this is a paid hospital position).
- Write a summary letter to the hospital authorities (CEO).
- Call your provincial hospital association.
- Contact your provincial College of Physicians and Surgeons. View their mandate, the status of a doctor and any complaints that may be registered against him, or lodge a complaint yourself online. (e.g. Ontario College of Physicians and Surgeons website at: http://www.cpso.on.ca/Info_Public/infopub.htm

- Contact the Royal College of Physicians and Surgeons of Canada (For specialists only) http://www.royalcollege.ca/index e.php)
  Or contact them directly at:
  The Royal College of Physicians and Surgeons of Canada
  774 Echo Drive, Ottawa ON. Canada K1S 5N8
  Telephone: 613-730-8177; toll free 1-800-668-3740
  Fax: 613-730-8830
  E-mail: info@rcpsc.edu
- In extreme circumstances you may contact the police and your lawyer.

Hopefully any concerns or misunderstandings can be resolved quickly and efficiently. If not, do not abandon your pursuit for a satisfactory explanation. While it may not affect your future care, other patients may be at risk should you decide to do nothing. Remember, an undocumented and unwritten complaint never happened! Nothing will change if you don't notify the hospital or clinic authorities in writing.

* * * * *

"Dirty hospitals kill 75,000 patients a year. Unnecessarily"

Michael J. Berens

Reader's Digest   •   February, 2003

"A report in today's New England Journal of Medicine estimates that sponges and other tools are left inside about 1,500 patients each year in the United States"

Andre Picard

The Globe and Mail• January. , 2003

"Errors occur and should be expected and anticipated"

Jan M. Davies

Canadian Medical Association Journal • Nov.. , 2001

A Little Insurance Goes A Long Way....

We've all heard the expression "Better safe than sorry". Nothing could be more appropriate when it comes to health care. Do yourself a favour and provide your family with a little insurance against unnecessary errors.

Protect Yourself

- Understand your illnesses and your options.
- Communicate as effectively as possible with those around you.
- Always bring a friend or family member for support.
- Educate yourself wherever and whenever possible.
- Get all the options.
- Take the time to make the right (or at least careful) decisions.
- Maintain that healthy dose of skepticism.
- Ask, Ask, Ask.
- Be Confident and Secure (or shop elsewhere!).
- Know if your treatment option is preventative (prevents a possible illness), therapeutic (relieves pain) or curative (fixes your problem).
- Understand the difference between *necessary* and *appropriate.*
- Don't be afraid of the fact that requesting a second opinion might insult your doctor (why should he be insulted?).
- Record everything – you will otherwise forget the most important details!

We suggest you read the report "Building A Safer System" released by the National Steering Committee on Patient Safety. Take care of your own health care interests, and above all else, become a Priority Patient because everybody knows, a good offence is undoubtedly the best defense!

Keys To Using Medications Wisely

Most of us believe that we know how to use medications wisely, both over-the-counter and prescription. We believe this because it looks simple. It isn't. We try to obey common sense rules. We do our best. In doing so, we make a lot of mistakes! We keep track of our medications by labelling them "the red one" and "the white one", the names seem too difficult. We ignore dosage, taking too much of one and not enough of the other. We frequently don't know why we are taking the drug. We indiscriminately mix prescription medications with over-the-counter drugs and natural remedies, having no idea what the effects may be. We even swap medications with others. What is it that makes us do these silly things? Why are we so careless? How do we survive such 'medication madness'? The following keys will help you ensure that you are practicing safe and reasonable medication use.

Home Health - The Least You Should Know

Let's assume you are concerned about medication safety. Wherever you come in contact with medication, *be careful*! Begin implementing safety measures at the drug store, the emergency room, the doctor's office, the hospital, and the walk-in clinic. The best place to start is at home. You should follow a few general safety rules.

Medication Safety At Home – The Do's

- Keep all medication (over-the-counter and prescription) out of the reach of children.
- Read package labels and inserts for additional information.
- Keep medication in a place with a relatively stable temperature.
- Make certain all prescriptions are CLEARLY labelled.
- Be aware of possible serious side effects of each medication.
- Always ask if there are alternatives to medication.
- Buy all medication from the same pharmacy; the pharmacist then knows all your medications, and can advise you on potential drug interactions.
- Keep on hand a list of your medications; name and dosage.
- Use a pill reminder box and/or a daily medicine chart to keep track of multiple medications, dosages and schedules.
- Follow the prescription instructions exactly—including dosage and schedule.

These lists are not meant to be all-inclusive. Some medications have special instructions e.g. refrigeration.

Medication Safety At Home – The Don'ts

- Never alter the form of a medication without asking the pharmacist (i.e. crushing or mixing).
- Never change medication from the original bottle to another.
- Some medications are not compatible with alcohol consumption.
- Never keep prescriptions past their expiry date.
- Never use prescriptions for persons other than those for whom they were prescribed.
- Don't second-guess your doctor about the medication you do or do not need; always discuss questions with your doctor first.
- Never stop taking any medication because you feel better or worse.
- If there are side effects consult your physician.
- If you are pregnant (or planning to be) do not take prescription or over-the-counter medication without consulting with your physician!

Don't ever allow yourself to be prescribed a medication to which you have had a serious reaction in the past.

The only person who can effectively protect you from being prescribed a medication to which you have had a serious reaction in the past is you. To be safe, record the name and dose of the medication, and the specifics of the reaction in your health care diary. Do not forget this reaction occurred! Ask your doctor for help with these details. Never accept a new medication of any kind without first informing the prescribing physician of your drug allergies.

Be cautious! If you don't know or understand, ask! Minimize the number of medications you take. Remember, the more medications you take, the more side effects you may experience and the more difficult it becomes to identify which drug is at fault.

★★★★★

"Thirty-eight ADEs [adverse drug events - errors] occurred in 32 patients...10 cases occurred during hospitalization...Among these 38 ADEs, 22 were considered avoidable (57.9%); 20 of these were associated with therapeutic errors (inappropriate administration, drug-drug interactions, dosage error..."

Peyriere H. et al.
The Annals of Pharmacotherapy · January, 2003

First Aid At Home - Be Prepared!

You never know in advance when you will need to treat one of your family members for an emergency. BE PREPARED! Here is a suggested list of first-aid necessities.

Medicine Cabinet Must-Haves

- Rubbing alcohol or Hydrogen peroxide - for cleaning cuts
- Laxative - even the most regular people need this sometimes.
- Anti-diarrhea medication
- Cortisone cream - for itching and bites
- Allergy medication (antihistamines)
- Cough syrup
- Antacids
- Eye drops (saline solution)
- Hemorrhoid preparation
- Petroleum jelly (Vaseline)
- Tweezers
- Vapor Rub– for chest and nasal congestion
- Antiseptic cream - for minor scrapes and cuts
- Pain and fever relief medications, such as ASA and Acetaminophen
- First aid supplies, like bandages and gauz
- Thermometer

Although it may not fit in the cabinet, you may also find it useful to have available a heating pad/ hot water bottle, humidifier/vaporizer (cool mist), and ice/heat packs.

It's OK If I Double Up - It's All-Natural!

Never assume that non-prescription products are completely safe. It may not be in your best interest to ingest large quantities of natural therapies without consulting your doctor or pharmacist. This is one of the most dangerous assumptions you can make. Vitamins can be harmful if the recommended daily dosage is exceeded! If you are taking a large or regular dose of an herbal preparation of any kind, again, check with your doctor first. Grapefruit juice can negatively affect your prescription medications!

If you consult an herbalist or a homeopathic doctor, inform your medical doctor. Even though natural remedies are often safe, effective, and mostly free of side effects, they may affect or be affected by prescription drugs, camphor, menthol, eucalyptus, tea tree oil, etc. For example, some people cannot drink coffee while using homeopathic remedies. Alcohol and street drugs such as cocaine may also negatively impact traditional as well as homeopathic treatments. Some prescription drugs such as steroids and antibiotics may also be a problem if combined with natural remedies. Contact your herbalist or homeopath for a complete list of possible interactions, and always consult your doctor before combining any remedies with prescription medications.

Over - The - Counter Drugs (OTCs)

Over-The-Counter medications can be quite beneficial as long as you treat them with the same respect as your prescription medications. Take care and do not dispense them to your family without full knowledge of their usefulness and safety.

It can be difficult to make the right choices when purchasing any OTC medication. Cough and cold medications are no exception. These are easily available as non-prescription medications and therefore you need to be extra careful when taking them yourself or giving them to your children. You should ask your physician in advance if they recommend cough medicine and how to use it wisely. You should also consult your pharmacist when purchasing OTC medications of any kind. Be aware of the differences between the various preparations available. Gone are the days of one-medicine-cures-all!

Over-the-counter medications can have negative effects for certain groups of patients. Cough medicines (many different kinds) for example can cause problems in people with the following conditions (this list is not all-inclusive):

-Brain disease
-Alcoholism
-Cystic fibrosis
-Colitis
-Diarrhea
-Diabetes
-Pregnancy

-Overactive thyroid
-Seizures
-Gallstones
-Drug induced central nervous system depression
-Are less than 2 years old

Your pharmacist may not only advise you which type of OTC you will find beneficial, but also may offer tips on when to take your medications, how to take them and possible side-effects. They may even advise you to seek medical help if your symptoms are severe or recurring. They are an excellent source of information regarding over-the-counter medications. The following are some pointers you should consider when purchasing or consuming OTC medications:

Over-The-Counter (OTC) Medications And Your Safety

- Ask your doctor about the OTC medications that you are using or plan to use.
- Ask which medications you should avoid.
- Do not exceed the dosage on the labels.
- Do not take OTC medicines on a regular basis (unless your doctor tells you it is ok to do so).
- Don't take *any* product if you are pregnant or nursing a baby unless your doctor agrees.
- Store all medications in a dry place, with a stable temperature.
- Keep your OTC medications out of children's reach.
- Don't *ever* tell children that medicine is candy (even if it helps them to take it more easily).
- Check the expiration dates frequently. Discard old medication properly (so it cannot be accessed by children) or return to a pharmacy.
- Check the ingredients on all OTC medications to ensure it does not contained a product you are allergic to.

Prescription Drugs - Make Certain You Get The Facts!

Prescription medications can be dangerous. It is reported that 10,000 hospitalized Canadians (100,000 Americans) die each year due to medical errors. This is the equivalent of a jumbo jet crashing approximately every five days! There is no reason to assume that this phenomenon is limited to North America.

Know your prescriptions. Have them explained to you more than once if necessary. Understand why you are taking them and what they do. Know the consequences of missing a dose or doubling a dose accidentally. Many medications are forgiving, others are not. Ask your doctor how necessary the medication is and how dangerous it is. Learn everything you can about your prescriptions; the knowledge may be very helpful to you in the future.

If you are unable to get a renewal of your prescription, it can be quite frightening. If you understand why and how your medications work, circumstances such as this may be less distressing. For example, some medications take a while to build up in your system before they become effective. Therefore, if you miss a dose or two, the body will still be benefiting from the amount already in your system. No need to panic! Another example is if you are taking a preventative medication. There is no guarantee that it is preventing the medical problem in the first place. Therefore you can probably miss a few doses safely. Indeed, most medications can be omitted for a few days to verify if you are having a negative reaction to them. Check with your doctor. In the case of accidental double dosing, there may or may not be a problem. Find out in advance how potentially dangerous your medications are if taken by the wrong person or in the wrong dose.

*****

"Many hospital admissions of elderly patients for drug toxicity occur after administration of a drug known to cause drug-drug interaction. Many of these interactions could have been avoided"

David N Juurlink et al.
Journal of the American Medical Association · April, 2003

Prescription Drugs - Make Certain Others Get The Facts!

If you must rely on someone else (e.g. teacher, homecare nurse, or babysitter) to administer medication to a family member, always make sure the label on the bottle is correct. Write out the instructions in full, and physically demonstrate exactly how much is to be given. Never assume others understand what you mean when it comes to prescriptions. BE CLEAR! If possible, have your doctor adjust medication times such that outside help is not required to administer medications. If your child requires medication during the day, ask your doctor if it can be adjusted to a 'before and after school' schedule for simplicity and your peace of mind! If there is any doubt in your mind about your elderly parents ability to safely take their own medication, get involved! Older patients are much more likely to make medication errors.

Be A Team Player - Take Notes!

Medication mastery (competently handling medications safely) is achieved by educating yourself and others and keeping your health care team involved. Record all medications in your personal health diary and keep these records current. Note why and how long you are taking them. Record any side effects that you experience while taking every prescription. Be informed and keep others informed!

"It is not rocket science. It doesn't cost anything, if you think about it. All the pieces are there already, it is just co-ordinating the pieces"

Dr. Hui Lee
The Medical Post · September, 2001

★ ★ ★ ★ ★

Chapter Summary

☞ **You must remember your drug allergies - It's dangerous to forget!**

☞ **Know everything there is to know about your medications!**

☞ **Understand how they work and why!**

☞ **Never take anything without discussing it with your doctor!**

☞ **Inform your doctor of any home remedies or alternative therapies that you are taking!**

☞ **No medication of any kind should be considered totally harmless!**

☞ **Don't trust anyone else to administer medications to loved ones unless you are 100% certain they understand what they are doing!**

☞ **If it isn't labelled, don't take it!**

☞ **Be aware; Stay alive!**

"It has been pointed out cynically, but perhaps correctly, that the only person qualified to give fully informed consent to an orthopedic procedure is an orthopedic surgeon"

Dr. Aamir Zubairy
The Medical Post · March, 2002

"While 76% of the 96 respondents were able to describe their operation and 71% recall the type of anesthetic, only 20% remembered the name of the surgeon. About 97% remembered having signed a consent document, but only 19% had actually read it. On average, patients remembered about 37% of their procedure's potential complications"

Andrew Skelly
The Medical Post · March, 2003

Keys To Completing The Legal Paperwork

No one looks forward to obtaining and completing legal documents. Legal paperwork of any kind can be anxiety provoking. Perhaps this is the reason many people procrastinate and find themselves faced with this task at the last minute. If you wait until you are critically ill, it may even be impossible. These documents represent your instructions regarding extremely important personal and health care issues. They can have significant implications whether you are completing them for yourself or a loved one. They should be completed at a time when you are relaxed, your thoughts are clear and you are prepared to make serious decisions regarding life and death issues. Some people prefer to make personal decisions of this magnitude on their own. Others involve their loved ones since they are intimately connected with the purpose of these documents.

Everyone has a different level of comfort when dealing with these important issues. Even well informed people may forget to create a last will and testament. Many people probably don't understand the meaning of such terms as *Advance Health Care Directive* and *Power of Attorney*. The Priority Patient recognizes the problems created by not making important life decisions and taking time to complete the proper legal documents. She also recognizes the burden placed on others (loved ones and friends) if they are suddenly handed the responsibility of making these profound decisions. As the authors, we do not claim any legal expertise. However, in this chapter we felt it important that you be introduced to some legal concepts and terminology. Who will decide if at death, you are to donate an organ? When will you decide how your estate is to be divided, when you are sick or when you are well? Will you decide in advance if you wish to be put on life support or leave this decision to a distraught loved one? There are many other similar questions. When and how you answer them is a very personal issue. We recommend two things; obtain the appropriate legal advice and make decisions before you are no longer able.

Legal Documents

1) Informed consent

Many steps in your medical care require that you indicate *in writing* your understanding of and agreement with what is to be done, the potential complications and the implications of the medical intervention. This is usually accomplished by signing a standard document entitled "Consent Form" on which the details are recorded. Examples are consents for surgery, diagnostic tests and participation in research trials. Do not sign without having this form explained to you in detail by an experienced and qualified person! Many patients sign this type of document without even reading it!

2) **Power of Attorney**

The Power Of Attorney (POA) is a document that you can sign where by you (the grantor) appoint someone (referred to as the attorney) to be your delegate or representative who can make legal decisions on your behalf if you are incapable of making those decisions by reason of disability or, in some cases, absence. The position of an 'attorney' is a position of trust and the attorney has a legal responsibility to act with integrity and to carry out the wishes of the person who appoints him/her. There are two separate and distinct Powers of Attorney that can now be prepared. *The Continuing Power Of Attorney For Property* can be defined as a general Power of Attorney giving the attorney either wide-raging or more specific powers over the assets of the person who grants it. This document may be limited as to extent of powers, specific time periods and other matters. *The Power of Attorney for Personal Care* appoints someone to make personal care decisions for the grantor when the grantor is unable due to mental incapacity. These can include such matters as health care, nutrition, shelter, clothing, hygiene, safety, consent or refusal of consent to treatment to which the *Health Care Consent Act, 1996*, or any successor legislation applies, and cessation of continuation of measures whereby her life may be artificially prolonged. Frequently, *advance health care directives* or *living wills* (see below) are included in the Power of Attorney for Personal Care. This is a complex process and we suggest that competent legal advice be obtained.

3) **Last Will And Testament**

Your *Last Will and Testament* defines for you and your loved ones and society at large, how you wish your assets to be handled upon your death. A properly prepared will can avoid many problems. In the absence of a will, these problems and legal implications can be profound. For example: 1) The legislature has provided that certain persons, determined by their relationship to you, can apply to be administrator of your estate 2) In the absence of a will, who your beneficiaries are is also set out by law 3) In certain instances, the Public Guardian and Trustee can become involved in the administration of your estate. These circumstances may very well not be in accordance with your wishes. It is imperative that legal assistance be obtained in the preparation of your will and it is sometimes wise to obtain input from a good financial advisor as well.

Legal Decisions / Health Care Directives

The established legal documents noted briefly above unfortunately may not encompass all of the various issues that can arise in our increasingly complex society. There are many issues in your health care that you will consider and reconsider. You should decide and formally document your wishes in advance and disclose them to your loved ones. Your health care team should also be aware of decisions you have made regarding certain aspects of your health care. Without this knowledge you may be exposed to unwanted medical care. These *Advance Health Care Directives* or *Living Wills* can be as simple or as complex as you wish and serve to personalize your health care. All of these can be included in your *Power of Attorney for Personal Care*.

1) Do Not Resuscitate

This concept has been around for a long time but only formalized in Canada in the last fifteen years. The *Do Not Resuscitate* order (DNR) which must be signed by a physician is specifically designed to identify a patient who has expressed their wishes not to be brought back to life in the event of an expected demise due to a disease process that is not going to improve. The ease with which such an order is written can vary from place to place and time to time, but requires the approval of the patient, the physician and the family. These written orders are used when a patient is in a hospital or nursing home. Some jurisdictions allow their use for patients who are living at home for the benefit of homecare and ambulance personnel. This do or do not resuscitate type of order is in many cases an oversimplification of what the patient is actually requesting. The concept of *Limitations on Treatment* has become much more widespread and requires much more than a 'yes' vs. 'no' approach.

2) Limitation On Treatment

If you know for sure that you will never want an autopsy performed on your body, you should so state in advance. If you wish to put specific limitations on your health care, it is wise to communicate these to your loved ones and health care team before you are unable to do so. If you never wish to receive a transfusion of blood products make it known. If you want to be resuscitated in certain circumstances but do not wish to be put on life support systems, you must convey this to your health care providers. All of this needs to be recorded, signed, dated and witnessed. A Priority Patient keeps a copy in their health care diary and gives a copy to their personal physician.

3) Organ Donor

In the situation of your imminent death, you may wish to donate portions of your body for the use of others. Obviously this decision is best made in advance. You can specify that this be for purposes of transplantation and/or scientific research. You may limit which organs are to be taken. You must document your willingness to be an organ donor. One way is by signing the appropriate portion of your driver's license. It is also possible to obtain a separate wallet card to carry in case of accidental death.

Chapter Summary

- Make sure you know exactly what's involved before giving any Informed Consent!

- Power of Attorney is a position of *trust*.

- Without a Last Will and Testament anything can happen!

- Advance health care directives allow you to *personalize* your care!

- Good legal *advice* is worth every dollar!

- Write it down, date it, sign it and get it witnessed!

- Periodically reassess your decisions; things change!

- A legal document isn't any good if it can't be found!

- Take charge of your future!

Keys To Medical Insurance

What is medical insurance? Insurance of any kind is complex; it is easy to buy a policy, but how do you know you are getting the right one? Why indeed are you buying the insurance? What are you trying to ensure? Your Health? Your well-being? Your diseases? Your employment? The cost of medical insurance increases as you get older and disease prone. There are many insurance companies with many different types of policies. These policies have too many clauses and a lot of fine print. Many of us don't take the time to *fully* understand the details and run the risk of purchasing the wrong policy. Worse still, we may be insured for the wrong thing and if we have made a mistake on the application form, the entire policy may be void and we forfeit our coverage.

What Kind Of Medical Insurance Are You Shopping For?

Many people do not understand the variety of medical insurance available. We list here six types of insurance with a medical component. They all consider a person's medical status at the time of purchase or cover the individual for specific medical events that occur while owning the policy. Disability, critical illness and travel are pertinent to our discussion here regarding medical insurance because they focus on illness rather than death.

Insurance Types

- Life
- Accidental Death and Dismemberment
- Credit Card (Accident)
- Disability
- Critical Illness
- Travel

Over the years, the basic categories of medical insurance have remained the same. The cost of a policy is generally dictated by the amount of insurance coverage and the status of the individual patient purchasing the insurance. There are many different insurance companies, each of which adds value to their individual policies by including extra coverage or other benefits. It really pays to shop around! A good insurance agent can save you a great deal of time and effort. I chose an agent who is an independent and can therefore search all companies for the policy that is most suitable to my needs. Other agents may only be able to offer you what their company has available. There can be tremendous variations in both cost and benefits, whether life-long or short-term, individual or family. Do your homework!

It is not the purpose of this chapter to make you an expert on medical insurance and how to buy it. Most people have a variety of insurance coverage, which may or may not have a medical component. Regardless of the type of insurance you already have or plan to obtain, each policy should be explained in detail. Understand the *benefits* and *limitations* of every policy you review to ensure that you are properly covered.

Disability Insurance

Disability insurance is the one form of insurance coverage that everyone should own. The only requirement is that you have a stable income at the time you purchase the policy. This may not apply to many self-employed entrepreneurs whose income is not stable. There are policies that will consider business owners, but they must be able to prove (with income tax files, etc.) that they have maintained a certain level of income over a period of time. In other words, they must prove a "stable" income. For those who qualify for disability insurance, there are a few points to consider before you purchase.

Disability Insurance

- No disability benefits are paid beyond age 65!
- Your benefits may or may not be taxable!
- Know the specific definition of 'disability' in your policy. Does it state able to return to your 'own' occupation or 'any' occupation?
- Know the definition of 'total' vs. 'partial' disability. Does it state able to return to 'some' vs. 'all' prior activities?
- You can purchase 'top-up extension' policies that pay benefits prior to and after your group policy benefits.
- Know the duration of your benefits – group policies often only cover up to two years.
- Know the waiting period before benefits begin; choose a policy with a time period suitable to you.
- You can be paid benefits on only 75% of your previous total income no matter how many policies you buy. Don't over-ensure yourself – you cannot collect on them all!

What you are planning for is income replacement to cover a period of disability. The most important concepts to consider when purchasing disability insurance are the different types (personal or group) and the different definitions for *disability* and *partial disability* with each policy. Know what these terms mean to you. Only a reliable insurance agent can clearly explain the variable definitions of disability in each policy. Only you can decide if the definition suits your individual needs.

Read the fine print!!!

Critical Illness (C.I.) Insurance

It is now possible to purchase a new type of insurance called 'Critical Illness Insurance'. You are insuring yourself in the event that you develop certain diseases. This type of insurance is unique in that even the unemployed can purchase it. There is no need to prove stable income – just good health! It is still possible to purchase this insurance if you or your family have a history of medical problems. Your premiums and benefits will depend on your specific history. This type of insurance (with it's lump sum payment should you develop the disease) can help you cover the costs associated with the development of a specific illness such as cancer, heart attack, etc. Each policy will have a different list of illnesses that are covered. You must survive the diagnosis for a specified period of time in order to receive payment. Here are some points to remember regarding Critical Illness Insurance.

Critical Illness Insurance

- Various policies cover different diagnoses (know the list).
- Currently benefits of these policies are nontaxable (this may change).
- Anyone can purchase critical illness insurance.
- Cost of premiums are based on medical and family history.
- In some cases if you die before the waiting period for payment your estate is refunded the premiums.
- It is a "lump sum" payment and does not continue paying benefits.

As always, you must read the details of the policy and understand exactly what you are buying. Know what is covered, what the definitions are, and most importantly what could void your policy. Even if you already have disability insurance, you can collect both disability and critical illness benefits. Since the law concerning Critical Illness insurance is relatively new (currently a tax free benefit), they may change in the future.

Medical Travel Insurance

The usual travel insurance provided by your credit card company is an *accident* insurance that pays out if an accident occurs. The specifics vary from card to card. These are not designed as medical travel insurance policies. Should you become *ill*, if you are *attacked* or have an accident while *engaging in any risky activities* such as parasailing, you are likely not covered!

Your current credit card company may offer supplemental medical travel insurance which you can purchase. Whether purchasing through your credit card, traditional insurance company, travel agent, or other source, here are some points to consider.

Purchasing Medical Travel Insurance

- Know the claims process and how long it takes.
- Age, length of trip and health status are all determinants of insurability and cost.
- Are your belongings covered for the return home (how about your spouse)?
- Whether you buy a 'per trip' or annual policy, purchase the maximum coverage you can afford.
- If buying a 'per-trip' policy, purchase as close to departure as possible to avoid cancellation hassles.
- Have access to a cash deposit for emergency medical care ($2000.00 US if possible).
- Acts of war are not covered by your insurance.
- Your policy can easily be voided by misrepresenting your health status.
- Inform your agent about any risky activities that you may undertake while away (e.g. Parachuting).
- If you have a pre-existing medical condition, know the limitations stated in your policy with regard to; disease stability, changes in medications and diagnosis, etc.

We cannot in this short communication inform you of *all* of the intricacies of *all* insurance policies. Insurance contracts are not mutually inclusive or exclusive. You may want to look into 'packages' that incorporate all of your insurance needs at a reduced rate. This is often beneficial when purchasing medical travel insurance, trip cancellation insurance, multi trip annual, travel accident insurance, car rental damage, flight interruption, baggage and general travel insurance, etc. The package is usually more economical and offers broader coverage. Investigate all of the possibilities and your specific requirements with a knowledgeable professional insurance agent before you decide on your personal package.

With All Medical Insurance Policies

CAUTION! Read and re-read your policy; understand your policy and have your insurance advisor explain the policy to you *in detail*. Ask as many questions as you can; you don't want to find out half way around the world that you are on your own! If a paid consultant's advice is necessary – GET IT!

Chapter Summary

- Have the policy explained in detail before you buy!

- Thoroughly consider your reasons for purchasing insurance in advance.

- Review your policies annually to ensure they are providing the coverage you need!

- If it sounds to good to be true, it probably is!

- Tailor your policies to reflect your family situation and changes.

- Medical travel insurance requires that you be *absolutely* honest about your medical status and any changes that occur before departure.

- Buy new policies before your next birthday to take advantage of lower premiums.

- NEVER miss a payment (or it jeopardizes your policy)!

- Know the toll free number and emergency hotline of your insurance company – carry it with you.

Keys To Health And Travel

In planning a vacation, a lot of thought goes into deciding where and when to go, how long you will be gone, what to pack and who will take care of things while you're away. But how much thought is put into preparing your medical supplies. For most of us, very little. Recognize that emergencies can occur when away on holidays or business trips. Don't be caught in a foreign country without;

- A health care diary
- Adequate medications
- Adequate health and accident insurance
- A strategy to continue necessary personal health care
- A willing physician contact at home
- A contingency plan if your condition changes

It is good advice to check with your physician before you travel particularly if you plan to be away for a prolonged period or if you are planning unusual activities or visiting unusual destinations (skydiving or climbing Everest!). He can advise you if it is wise or even safe for you to travel and if there are certain restrictions on your activities. He will also ensure you have an adequate amount of the right medications. Always ask if you can call him if you run into trouble while away.

Getting Suggestions Elsewhere

There are many opportunities for you to seek travel advice. Travel agents, travel brochures, airlines and websites are all potential sources of information. Find out if you need to be vaccinated. This will depend on your destination. Perhaps the easiest source for most travellers is the local government Public Health Unit. There are also excellent resources on the internet that provide detailed information about worldwide destinations as well as general common sense travel tips.

Site Seeing

- **CDC Travellers' Health** - http://www.cdc.gov/travel/
  The National Centre for Infectious Diseases. This site includes information on outbreaks, specific diseases, recommended vaccinations, as well as general information about travelling with children and pets.
- **Travel Health Online** - http://www.tripprep.com/
  Health and safety information for travellers. This site answers questions about immunizations and disease risks by specific country.
- **International Society of Travel Medicine-** http://www.istm.org/ An organization of professionals dedicated to the advancement of the specialty of travel medicine.
- **Travel Doctor** - http://www.traveldoctor.co.uk/Info.htm
  Provides tips for travellers, many information pages, disease and immunization information, insect and animal bites, exposure, and information regarding many vacation-specific health issues (scuba, mountain climbing, etc.).

Being Prepared - What On Earth Will You Bring???

It is difficult to predict what you might encounter while travelling. Remember, if it can go wrong at home, it can go wrong on a trip (when it is much more inconvenient). In addition to the advice given by your doctor and other sources, consider the following list of items to take on any trip.

Essentials For Your Trip

- Your personal health care diary
- A note from your doctor with a medical diagnosis for a chronic condition
- Enough of each medication in your carry on bag
- Enough medication to last your whole trip. Take extra with you in case of theft or delay.
- Other supplies as required (e.g. needles, syringes, colostomy or incontinence supplies)
- The name and phone number of your doctor
- The name and dosage of each medication
- Multivitamins
- Medical ID bracelet (diabetes, epilepsy, blood thinner, etc.)
- Extra eyeglasses, contact lens solutions (What will you do if you lose them - Do you have a copy of the prescription?)

- Extra hearing-aid batteries
- Sunscreen (SPF 15 or higher)
- Insect repellent
- Paper supplies (i.e. feminine hygiene products, diapers, tissue, band aids)
- Your own pillowcase for use in hotels
- Sufficient cash for out of pocket expenses
- Travel insurance information
- Water purification tablets

First-Aid

It is also a good idea to keep a basic first-aid kit handy for those unexpected emergencies. Equip your own or purchase a ready made unit. Some of our recommendations are: bandages, scissors (not on board!), tweezers, thermometer, throat lozenges, antiseptic, motion sickness medication, cough medicine and allergy relievers, antihistamine, pain reliever, antacid, over-the-counter anti-diarrhea product and something for fever. Some websites will offer to prepare this for you with specialty items depending on your destination. Remember, you can never be too careful, or anticipate too many problems. If it can happen to you, rest assured it will! A Priority Patient can turn a potential medical disaster into a minor nuisance by being prepared!

Air Travel And Other Sources Of Motion Sickness...

Whether travelling by plane, car, boat or train, "motion sickness" can strike anyone. Visual stimuli (moving horizon), poor ventilation (smoke, fumes) and emotional factors (fear, anxiety) commonly act with motion to precipitate an attack of motion sickness. Symptoms may consist of cold sweating, hyperventilation, pallor, dizziness, headache, fatigue, weakness, nausea, and vomiting. Here are some tips on coping with motion sickness:

Coping With Motion Sickness

- Position yourself where the motion is least (e.g. middle of the ship, close to water level, over-the wings in a airplane).
- Avoid visual fixation on moving objects such as waves.
- Avoid reading.
- A semi-recumbent position with the head supported is best.
- Good ventilation is important.
- Avoid alcohol or dietary excesses before or during travel.
- Earplugs also may help.

Dealing With Prolonged Flights

Air travel can impose important medical and environmental challenges. It can cause or worsen existing medical conditions. However, only a few medical conditions prohibit air travel. Priority Patients plan and take precautions. Some examples of problems that can occur are listed below.

Jet Lag – A disruption of normal body (circadian) rhythms related to a change in exposure to daytime/night-time lighting created by travel through multiple time zones. Note, travel East to West is different from West to East.

Venous Thrombosis – Blood clots can occur in the leg veins of travellers sitting for prolonged periods. Infrequently, these clots can break off and move to the lungs.

Disrupted Medication Schedules – Some treatment schedules must be altered to compensate for changes in body rhythms and/or day/night timing.

Psychological stress – Fear of flying and/or claustrophobia (fear of small places) can precipitate symptoms such as hyperventilation and anxiety.

Barometric pressure changes – Depending on the type of aircraft, cabin pressure may aggravate certain medical conditions e.g. sinusitis, otitis media (ear infection), etc.

Communicable diseases – Passengers are in extremely close quarters with large numbers of people breathing re-circulated air.

Oxygen tension – Certain patients with severe lung or heart disease may require supplemental oxygen during flight.

Pregnancy – Pregnant women (after 36 weeks) or those with high risk pregnancies should consult their physicians regarding air travel to evaluate individual level of risk. Pregnant women are at higher risk of forming blood clots in the legs.

Special Requests and Devices – Patients with special needs and/or devices may require additional assistance and should discuss individual circumstances with the airline.

Diet/Special Meals – Special foods including low-sodium, low-fat, and
diabetic diets are available if requested in advance. Allergy prone
patients must be especially careful!

Fainting – A common problem related to air and oxygen supply,
temperature, humidity and other environmental factors.

Air Travel Suggestions

- Get plenty of rest before you travel.
- To avoid dehydration drink nonalcoholic, decaffeinated beverages
and water.
- Avoid overeating and eat well-balanced meals.
- Use sleep-aids sparingly.
- Melatonin may help with jet lag (but use only on the advice of your
physician).
- Decongestant medication may relieve symptoms related to take-off
and landing (cabin pressure changes).
- Swallowing can relieve symptoms during take-off/landing.
- Babies can suck on a bottle or a pacifier during the flight.
- Get up and move about during your flight (unless the crew tells you
not to – it may prevent blood clots in your legs).
- If prescribed, wear support stockings.
- Notify airline of specific dietary requirements in advance.
- A sedative before the flight may relieve anxiety (ask your M.D.).
- Be prepared to adjust your medication schedule.
- Make special arrangements for wheelchairs, oxygen or other
assistance in advance.

Don't hesitate to ask the airline or travel agent any questions you have
regarding travel. If you require oxygen on your trip, the airline will provide
it for you (at a cost). Federal air regulations do not allow you to carry your
personal oxygen unit on board. Don't forget to make arrangements for lay-
overs between flights. If you require wheelchair services, contact the airline
well in advance and re-confirm the arrangements at a later date before you
leave. Did you know that it is dangerous to fly within 24 hours of scuba
diving? Ask your doctor or diving authorities for guidelines on flying after
scuba diving. Priority Patients are well prepared for travel. Be safe and
Have fun!

Chapter Summary

- Always consult your doctor before going on a trip if you have any medical concerns.

- Travel creates loss of routine – Patients beware !

- Your health care diary is essential since you are a stranger while away.

- Medical services away from home may be different.

- If you need medical supplies at home, you need medical supplies while away!

- Assume that where you are going is nothing like home!

- Take extra medications with you and keep some in two separate places (e.g. carry on and suitcase) in case of loss or theft.

- What will you do if you lose your pills or eyeglasses?

- Is your doctor going to be on holidays while you are on holidays?

Secrets About Your Health Record

You have too many! Your multiple medical encounters have created multiple health records. All of them are incomplete. Remember, they are designed for the use of the professionals and institutions that hold them. They are not connected. If they were, there would exist a single, large, complete health record for each patient. Such does not exists. It is unlikely that it will in the future. Where would it be held and who would be responsible for it? Good questions. You can appreciate that if you want a single comprehensive health record, *you* are the only one who can create it and keep it current.

We are living longer today and because we are older we have more medical problems. It is impossible for us to remember all the dates, names of physicians, clinics, hospitals, medications, drug reactions, surgeries, etc. In many cases, the lost information won't be missed. However, in some cases it will. "Was that a partial or total hysterectomy?" "Did I have 3 or 4 coronary bypasses?" "I think they told me in the emergency room that I had heart disease". "Was I supposed to take this for 2 more months or 2 more weeks?" Try as they may, people cannot remember *all* of these important health care details. Patients with diseases such as diabetes, high blood pressure and heart or kidney disease will have a multitude of medication changes, diagnostic tests and interactions with a variety of health care professionals during the course of these life-long illnesses. Who's to remember the details? Can it be done? Does it really matter?

Let's imagine that you are 65 years of age and have seen 14 physicians throughout your lifetime: two surgeons, four emergency medical doctors and three different hospital admissions. There now exists segments of your medical record in many files and many doctors only have pieces of your puzzle. You have 23 incomplete health/medical records. Each contains potentially important information that may affect your well being but they are not being shared!

The Problem With Multiple (Incomplete) Records

Patients today are thankful for the excellent care they *eventually* receive. They are not necessarily pleased with *how* the care is provided. They recognize and are frustrated by the needless repetition each time they see a new physician, nurse or therapist. How often do you have to answer the same questions? Surely you should be able to give your medical history once and then add to it rather than starting from the beginning each time. Except in the case of your physician-partner, every new medical encounter assumes you have never been questioned or examined before. You are handled like a stranger! Each new encounter is considered an isolated event. Minimal if any consideration is given to the context in which that event occurred. A document is created. These documents may or may not reach your familiar health care professionals. They are the property of and stored by the various locations you have visited over the years. Welcome to fragmentation stranger!

Today, it is less common that a patient has a single personal physician. Indeed hundreds of thousands of Canadians have no personal physician at all! After hours, nights, weekends and holidays, none of us have an accessible personal physician. The result is, we seek our medical care in a variety of non-traditional health care outlets. This is now common practice for most of us. It is not unusual for a patient to be seen for health care at several different locations in the course of a year. They may be seen once or several times at each of these outlets. If follow-up care is suggested it may not be done or done at another outlet. There exists an assumption that the patient will go to their family physician for follow-up care. The personal physician rarely receives any formal documentation regarding these events. There is little or no communication between these various health care outlets. Even so, each of them must maintain a file. If the patient was hospitalized, there may be attempts to send copies of reports to the family physician but these frequently fail and are certainly not deemed a priority. It remains the patient's responsibility to communicate the outcome of these visits to their personal physician.

Even in the event that a physician refers a patient to a specialist, the specialist may receive no more than a cryptic note saying something such as "Chest pain - please evaluate". Frequently, the personal physician's *segment* of the patient's medical record is not available to the specialist. The specialist must make an effort to obtain the necessary information about the particular patient from numerous sources. Now the specialist has created yet another *segment* of your medical file! All this disconnected record-keeping activity is time consuming, fragmented and leads to repetition and misunderstandings. How often has an important health care decision been made without all the necessary information? How much time did it take the last health care professional who assessed you (as a stranger) to make an important decision regarding your treatment? How many minutes were spent on: your present illness, previous illnesses, operations, allergies, immunizations, medications (new and old), family history, advance directives, emotional state, recent exposures? Your health is far too important to leave to chance, best guesses and sketchy memories.

"My office nurse spends half of her time attempting to find bits and pieces of missing patient information from a variety of sources
- we never know for sure if we have it all or not"

RSB

Why Is Now The Time?

You are now aware that there is a growing number of people who suffer from chronic illnesses as opposed to acute illnesses. *Chronic* illness (heart disease) is long lasting and incurable. It is characterized by periodic clinical events requiring a management strategy consisting of recurrent diagnostic testing and changing treatment. *Acute* illness (appendicitis) is abrupt in onset and usually short term. It is characterized by isolated clinical events requiring specific diagnosis and frequently curative therapy.

The multiple interactions with the health care system created by chronic illness creates the need for a health care tracking system that not only describes the illness but also its evolution over time. The fragmentation of health care delivery currently witnessed in the system today is not conducive to the creation and maintenance of a single health care record (tracking system). Monitoring and recording the *progress* of an individual with a chronic illness is one of the many benefits offered by a doctor/patient partnership. Such a tracking system is not found in a 'piece work' environment of fragmented care and record-keeping. Wouldn't it be nice if each patient had their own 'health care passport' to be presented each time they encountered the medical establishment. Such does not exist!

Any patient can improve their level of participation in the medical care they receive. Practice makes perfect! Your diary will improve as confidence is gained and your level of comfort improves. I believe your physician/partner will work closely with you in this exercise to not only improve your personal health tracking system but also your involvement in and understanding of your health issues. It may one day provide the necessary clues to helping you with an illness event in the future. Even children may benefit since life threatening illnesses such as penicillin allergy can occur very early in life and should never be forgotten!

If you create your own personal health diary you can take it with you each time you interact with the health care establishment. You will be able to hand each health care professional you interact with your complete medical history so that they have instant access to vital information; no mistakes, no omissions, no assumptions, just the straight health life facts about you and your problem.

★ ★ ★ ★ ★

"So much of [health care] is an information transaction, so to speak"

Dr. David Lansky
American College of Cardiology "Practice News" · Jan.,2003

The Future Of Health Care Records

Suggesting that patients take *responsibility* for tracking their health records is revolutionary. It would be *irresponsible* to suggest that complete documentation of all important medical events be handled by patients. You may not necessarily have all of the pathophysiological details in your diary, but you are the 'reference librarian'. You become the individual who knows what happened, when, where and who was involved. This alone is vital information that can be extremely useful to those involved in your care! They may have to go searching to expand on the details but thanks to you they are aware what events occurred and who to contact. You can not imagine the relief you offer an emergency room or walk-in clinic physician when you provide them with such information. You cannot imagine how much you improve your own safety!

Many efforts are being made by the establishment to consolidate patient records. Not only will this take a long time to occur but will not be successful without active patient participation. To date, patients have not participated in the record-keeping process in any meaningful way. This must change in the future! The Priority Patient will actively participate in every level of care: prevention strategies, record keeping, self-education, decision making and compliance with therapy. I believe the future will see the medical record as a document primarily concerned with the patient's well being and will no longer consist of fragmented segments of information held by physicians and institutions for medical/legal reasons alone. Patients and their physician/partners will recognize the importance of this approach and collectively work towards optimizing the availability of the most accurate and complete information possible.

The patient will become a more active participant. It will not matter that institutions continue to barely cope with the problems of information collection, storage and utilization. The patient should and will be the custodian of a personal health care record. The future will decide how this is accomplished. As for the present, the fastest way to becoming a Priority Patient is to create your own personal health diary.

Keys To Creating A Personal Health Diary

Everyone should maintain their own system for recording important personal health care information. It's so easy! You can call this new tool a personal health diary, personal health record, health care portfolio or even your health care passport. You can purchase a commercially available health care record keeping system or create your own. You decide. The important point is that you select the one that suits your needs and that you keep it accurate and up to date. It will become the single most effective means of ensuring your safety as well as improving the quality of the health care you receive. This personal health record encourages you to record and track important contacts, health care events and other pertinent information. The following pages should form the basis of any commercial or personally developed health care recording system. Although all systems will be similar, Priority Patients will personalize each of the pages to suit their individual needs.

Components Of A Personal Health Diary

Your diary may take any number of shapes and sizes. Simple sheets of lined paper with appropriate headings or even a small notebook with sections similar to those described below. You might even consider a few large labelled envelopes to securely hold specific documents as suggested. Don't forget to clearly identify yourself on each and every document. You are going to have this diary for a long time. Make sure you record your information in a manner that will not fade with time. It's not a bad idea to purchase very good quality paper (single sheets or book) and a sturdy portfolio or carrying case for ease of storage and transportation. Most commercial diaries will suggest the following sections for your convenience.

"My Personal Profile"

- Name and address
- Date of birth
- Phone, fax and email
- S.I.N. #
- Provincial health card number
- Height, weight and blood type
- Employer's name and phone
- Health insurance agent, phone and your policy number
- Emergency contact name and number
- All allergies (life threatening and other)
- All Immunizations/Vaccinations
- Other...

"My Advance Health Care Directives"

- Wishes regarding cardiopulmonary resuscitation
- Instructions regarding performance of autopsy
- Your decision regarding personal organ donation
- Religious restrictions on your care
- Power of attorney – name and phone
- Pre-arranged funeral instructions
- Date and location of your last will and testament
- Other...

"My Medications"

- List all current medications and dosages.
- List all previous medications and reasons for stopping.
- List all natural (alternative) therapies.
- List all medication allergies and how you became aware of them.
- List known possible drug interactions.
- Note special instructions for each medication.
- Other...

"My Family History"

- List diseases of immediate family members.
- List cause of death of immediate family members.
- In the event of a genetic disease in the family, you might create a family tree illustrating the impact.
- In the event that you are responsible for the care of a loved one create a separate health care diary with them.
- Other...

"My Medical/Surgical Events"

- List of all hospital admission and the reason
- List of all surgical procedures
- List of all serious medical illnesses
- List of all serious infections
- Physicians and surgeons involved
- Name and location of hospitals
- Description of all event outcomes
- Other...

"My Health Care Team"

- Family doctor (contact information such as: address, phone, email)
- Medical specialists (e.g. cardiologist, internist, pediatrician)
- Optometrist
- Surgical specialty (orthopedics, neurosurgery)
- Dentists, oral surgeon
- Chiropractor
- Alternative medical practitioner (homeopathic doctor, herbalist)
- Psychiatrist
- Pharmacist
- Physiotherapist
- Other...

'Unique' Components Of A Priority Patient's Diary

I believe that Priority Patients will want to participate in a fashion that requires some unique additions to the standard suggested health care diary. These additional sections will promote greater efficiency and better communication with your health care team. You are encouraged to save copies of important professional documents (even originals), such as specialist consultation notes, descriptions of surgical procedures and diagnostic test results. This will surely identify you as an individual who abhors needless and unnecessary repetition. You will quickly recognize the unique features of these added components.

"My Reasons To See The Doctor"

Remember the Big Bang! Priority Patients are prepared for their visit to the doctor. They create a 'symptom form' on which they record their symptom or complaint and describe it in as much detail as possible. They bring this written summary with them to facilitate the doctor's history taking process. Some examples of important details regarding a symptom can be illustrated by the example of chest pain. Where does it hurt? When did it start? How long did it last? Was it sharp, dull, pressing or burning? What seems to make it worse? What seems to make it better? Have you been treated for this before? If so, what was done? You may use this form to describe the outcome of your visit and future treatment plan. This form documents your personal 'Big Bang'; USE IT WELL!

"My Symptom Journal"

A Priority Patient will also create a symptom log or journal to keep an accurate record of symptoms, past, present and future. All patients tend to forget the details of past complaints and medical encounters. With such a form, important information regarding previous symptoms (e.g. headache, chest pain, diarrhea, etc.) is not lost with the passage of time as is frequently the case. It is unfortunate that such lost information is frequently the cause of present and future medical mishaps.

"My Medical 'Form' Letters"

Organized patients can assist their personal physician by being prepared in advance when confidential information must be exchanged. Signed authorization is required for your physician to release information on you to another medical facility. The same authorization is required for the reverse. Your physician may be required to sign a return to work, confirmation of treatment, or other similar formal documents. The Priority Patient has these forms prepared and completed in advance. This saves both the doctor and patient time and effort and maybe even money!

"My Archive Documents"

Actively participating patients recognize the importance of maintaining a file of specific professional documents and reports. Your health care professionals will be thankful when you are able to provide them with information that may otherwise not be available. Consider collecting and filing copies of health records including hospital discharge summaries, remote treatment reports, ER and clinic reports, test results, etc. It is unlikely that anyone else will maintain a file of information regarding assistive devices such as hearing aid type and model, prescription for corrective lenses, prosthetic devices (e.g. pacemakers, heart valves, artificial joints). This type of specific information can be of critical importance in emergency situations or with product recalls. Some of you may require receipts for medical expenses when submitting claims to insurance companies or using them for tax purposes (e.g. prescriptions, home oxygen, physiotherapy).

MY REASON(S)
TO SEE THE DOCTOR

personal health **diary**

Appointment date and time

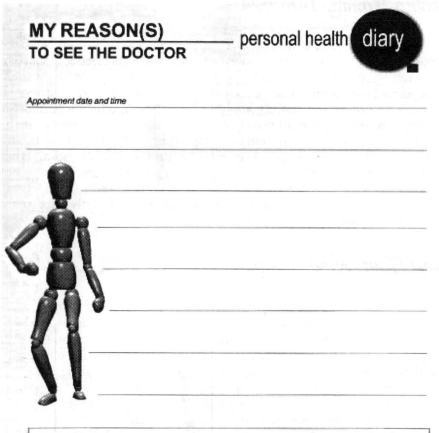

> *Remember to bring your health card, your medications, your health diary, any documents that may be required, and make sure your doctor has forwarded important information if you are going to a specialist.*

Please think about these questions as they might apply to your condition and make notes to share with the doctor.

What do you think is wrong? Where does it hurt? When did it start? How long did it last, or is it ongoing? What are the usual circumstances when this problem arises? What seems to make it worse? What seems to make it better? Have you had it before? If so, have you been treated for this before? What treatment did you try? What worked?

Result of my visit

My next appointment (Make sure to enter this information in your Health Diary.)

Reprinted with permission from www.personalhealthsystem.com, February 2003.

Keeping Family Informed

When you get sick your family is concerned. They want you to receive the best possible care. They want to know that your wishes are being respected. They do not want to have you under or over-treated. You do not want them to be burdened with unnecessary decision making. Your properly maintained health care record clearly states your specific wishes and instructions. This information must be promptly conveyed to your health care team in the greatest of detail to avoid any misunderstandings. Use your health care diary to remember all of the details of your health life. Tell your family that you have one. Take it with you for all health care encounters. In the event of an emergency ensure it is easily accessible. Your health care diary will help avoid an unnecessary situation in which the health care team responsible for your care is 'in the dark'.

Using Your New Passport With C'AIR Canada

If you never leave your home town, see more than one doctor, and never have an emergency involving unknown health care professionals, you will probably never need a health care passport. You won't be a stranger. However this is very unlikely! Most of us travel, change physicians, require emergency medical assistance and visit multiple health care outlets during our lives. When you do move about there are standard documents that you should carry with you. Your wallet usually contains photo I.D., driver's license, credit card and perhaps social insurance number. In some circumstances you may require your birth certificate or international passport. Why? Because you must be identifiable. If you carry a personal health diary (a form of health passport) you and your health care issues are immediately identifiable.

Involving Health Care Professionals

Your personal physician or specialist may respond unexpectedly to your record keeping efforts. Some doctors will think it is fantastic. Others might see it as a form of interference. None of them will expect you to be so well organized. The enlightened ones will review your records and likely request a copy for their file! Tell them how you got started, from where the idea came and how the diary has helped. Ask them to work with you to enhance the quality of information in your system. For example, they may provide you with copies of tests and reports. They may recognize other patients who would benefit from such a system.

Outlining The Benefits For Your Doctor

- Saves your doctor time and repetition (such as asking repeatedly if you have any allergies, what medications your are taking, your history, etc.)
- Negates the need to go back to the beginning
- Saves the nurse/secretary time tracking down information and test results
- Eliminates the hassle of having consent forms filled out to release information from other offices
- Serves as an accurate reminder of where and when tests were performed
- Provides them with a well thought out, written description of your symptoms
- Saves the time spent taking the history
- Provides a place for the doctor or nurse to write down the treatment plan as well as instructions to the patient
- Eliminates many patient phone calls to the office for missed information

Design your diary so that it is convenient for you to transport. When you arrive at a hospital emergency department or a walk-in clinic the staff and physicians should be thrilled that you have such detailed records. Remember you are a stranger! You cannot imagine the amount of time you save, tests you avoid and errors you prevent. I know that emergency room physicians will undoubtedly love it. It immediately provides information they desperately require. In this environment, time is of the essence. Just think of what a large number of Priority Patients could save the system in terms of time, money and effort! It's so easy!

The Benefits For Unfamiliar Health Care Professionals

- Provides a starting point for your chart
- Allows for all previous tests results to be in the file
- Reduces errors
- Raises their level of efficiency
- Avoids the need for consent and release of information forms
- Provides contact names and numbers of doctors, labs, etc.
- Provides a well thought out symptom form with which to begin
- Offers a place to write out the diagnoses and treatment plan (a form of communication with your family physician which is otherwise impossible)
- Avoids costly and time-consuming repetition

Involving Foreign Health Care Professionals

Priority Patients will recognize the need for a health care passport when they travel internationally. Under these circumstances, you should include information such as specific vaccinations received, potential medical contacts at your destination and detailed information regarding travel/medical insurance. Beyond a simple wallet card identifying your serious allergies, detailed information about your chronic medical conditions will definitely be required if your health status changes while abroad. For people who travel a lot, the health care passport may require a different format. The accessibility of a traditional 'paper' version of your health care diary may be less convenient than an electronic version saved on disk or CD. Some Priority Patients will utilize one of the new and innovative websites that allow for the creation of and confidential access to a complete electronic personal health care diary (e.g. www.personalhealthsystem.com).

Using Your Cyber Passport

Now and increasingly in the future greater numbers of patients will take advantage of the many conveniences offered by an electronic health care diary. With standard web access your diary can be easily created and updated from any location. Your confidential health information is easily viewed by you and those individuals and health care professionals to whom you have granted access. These electronic systems will vary in their sophistication and likely improve with time. If you are considering subscribing to one of these services find out if they provide the following benefits.

Unique Cyber Passport Benefits

- Upload of original documents (e.g. x-ray, test results, consult notes)
- A calendar function for tracking appointments, prescription renewal dates, etc.
- Customizable passwords which allow limited access to viewers
- New technology that allows automated email communication with your health care team (automated notices to your pharmacist regarding advance notice of prescription renewals)
- Printable forms for adding to your traditional paper diary

As with any other document that is designed to identify you as a specific individual with unique features, your health care diary (in any form) will define your individuality, ensure your health safety and secure your status as a Priority Patient!

Chapter Summary

→ **It's Easy!**

→ **Buy or build your own.**

→ **Make it durable and keep it safe!**

→ **Record all details accurately!**

→ **Keep your files up to date!**

→ **Tell your family where your diary is located!**

→ **Take it to every appointment!**

→ **Label in case it is misplaced.**

→ **Involve your health care team!**

Epilogue

The practice of medicine is changing. The doctor's role in the 'business of medicine' is evolving. Patients' expectations are changing, some less and some more demanding. Obviously, the medical establishment and the entire health care system are stressed to the breaking point. Resources, personnel, equipment, money.... all in apparent short supply. Certainly improved efficiencies abound, but there are not a lot of creative new ideas. It's almost a matter of too little, too late!

Where is it all going? Will we see longer line-ups, fewer insured services, shorter tempers, more lawyers? Will we see more mistakes? Maybe just the opposite. There may be a move to privatization (though unpopular), there may be a red carpet treatment for those who pay extra. Maybe the doctor patient relationship will become closer and more personal, not less so with the increased turn-style, drive-thru type of health care...NEXT!

I believe we will see a split in the system. Patients who get faster, better, more personalized care and the opposite. We will go through a phase of offering 'charter' or 'business class' medical service. In which group will you be, charter or business class? To a large extent it depends on you. I don't think it will simply depend on money. I think it will be the quality of the people (both doctors and patients) who enter into these relationships. By quality, I mean those who care! There will be more than one way to 'upgrade' your care from 'economy' to 'first class'. You can become a Priority Patient with your knowledge, behaviour and confidence or a combination of any of these qualities.

Whether you go charter (public) or business (private) you can reach priority status by showing you care, you are involved, you will participate in your care and the decisions required to make changes. Your behaviour will dictate your treatment. Your disease will be treated the same either way. Patients and doctors will want to have mutually satisfying and rewarding relationships. Not just drive-thru, à la carte treatment of today's problem, but rather valuable, long-term commitment, involving each other, affecting each other in ways that are rewarding beyond the economics.

Doctors strive to help patients solve their health care problems and get better, particularly if the patients show an interest too! Patients want a doctor to care about them and give them suitable advice. They need to trust that advice and the person from whom it came. Today, there are too many errors and far too much superficial caring. It's hard to get anything more meaningful from the assembly line environment that we have become accustomed to using and abusing daily. We all want something better. We all support the current system because we are afraid of change. However, change could be better for everyone. Right now, I encourage you to involve yourself, identify yourself every time you encounter a health care professional. You must! In years to come, when relationships improve, it may not be necessary, but it most definitely is now!

The Priority Patient will avoid uncertainty, ensure communication and actively participate in her care. She will minimize risk, discard repetition, and abhor inefficiency in all its forms. The Priority Patient will contribute to the health care system like never before! In doing so, she will assume her rightful place as the centre of the health care universe, being orbited by all the components of health care. The knowledgeable and confident patient will revolutionize their care by active participation, understanding the strengths and weaknesses of health care and minimizing their own risk.

When you are sick and in need of help, the system will be there. You can decide right now if you are going to be treated as a stranger or as a Priority Patient. The system is there to help you with your problems. If you can avoid contact with the system...do so! Instead of blindly and indiscriminately asking for and receiving more 'off the rack' tests, more operations, more medications, and more 'quick fixes', ask for and receive what you have always wanted: personalized, made to measure, customized advice and treatment designed for each individual.

This treatment will be delivered by a 'team' chosen by you; selected for your specific personality, character, philosophy, life situation, medical problem and social responsibilities. Together you and your team will assess, investigate and manage your symptoms and medical problems in a partnership designed to maximize the outcome for your benefit. Your health care advisors will be chosen for their long-term commitment, expertise, and their ability to communicate in a way you understand and appreciate. With your guidance they will minimize repetition, optimize appropriate care and maximize, not the quantity, but rather the quality of your health care.

In the present 'no competition' medical environment, health care services represent a 'seller's market'. With limited personnel and resources, line-ups and waiting lists, the last thing any medical professional or administrator wants to see in this 'health care business' is another patient! This will change! It must! The current lack of resources and competition has already led to fragmented, walk-in care. Legislated physicians, salaried nurses, incommensurable hospital administrators, revolving government officials all demonstrate and perpetuate the legacy of our current system.

You will be responsible (as you are now) for what you have, what you get and how your health care is delivered in the future. But you must act to initiate change and to 'prioritize' yourself. Upgrade your health insurance card to 'platinum'. If the American system can be said to be driven by profit, the Canadian system has been driven by coping. The future will bring not only kudos to hospitals that perform, but budget increases (bonuses) to those whose performance is measured in positive patient outcomes and results rather than by strict adherence to budget; people, not just economics!

STOP thinking about your health care as if it were a seatbelt, an airbag, a roll bar or a crash helmet. Health care is not just a safety net! START considering health care as a component of life. You do your part; the medical establishment will do its part when required. If you develop an illness (chronic most likely) you continue to do your part by: responding, recording, monitoring, and participating in the treatment strategies and solutions. The future is already here for those who have chosen to prioritize themselves in the eyes of the establishment, as equals, expecting the appropriate (not the most!) health care, and making informed choices based on best advice and their personal beliefs.

These are the early ones who are frequently unappreciated. They are the 'test pilots'. Remember, the medical establishment is evolving. It may not appear ready or prepared for 'Priority Patients', but once informed, it will welcome them, work with them, and enjoy what they bring to the table. You will be given the attention you request. You will be respected and you will become 'special'. You must earn this new position. You must learn, you must participate, and you must live with your choices! You will become the centre of your personal health care universe. That universe is vast, impressive, awesome, and overwhelming. Make it work *for* you and *with* you!

Contrary to much contemporary thought, patients are not the enemy. They are our troops and should be treated as such. Yes patients can be demanding and are frequently difficult. However, they are the sole purpose and driving force for the existence of the system. If they look, sound or act like the enemy it is because the medical establishment has created that attitude. Many patients have become subservient, dependant and insecure when exposed to the medical establishment.

Now is the time for change. Together, patients and health care workers are fighting for better health care, education, communication, and appreciation of what can be accomplished together. Patients as members of the health care army are much better utilized when perceived as allies. The medical establishment can train them, advise them, educate them and enlighten them with far less resistance than previously experienced. Together we can achieve a higher standard of health care. We will all eventually want to become a Priority Patient.

Dr. Ronald S. Baigrie F.A.C.C., F.R.C.P.(C)

Medical School For Patients

Has Completed The First Stage of Becoming a Priority Patient

Dr. R. Baigrie - Founder

Date

Order Form

To purchase copies of the Priority Patient Book or the PHS Health Care Diary, complete this form and mail with cheque or money order to:

Medical School for Patients
65 Larch Street, Suite 200C
Sudbury, Ontario, Canada. P3E 1B8

Shipping Information:

Name:

_____

Address:

_____

_____

Phone #: _____

Total number of items requested: _____

Number of book copies requested: _____ X $19.95 CAN.   _____

Personal Health System Diary: _____   X $24.95 CAN. + _____

(Please add applicable tx [gst only for Book/gst +pst for diary] +$3.00 s&h)

Total payment enclosed: = $ _____

Note : Please make all cheques and money orders payable to:
Medical School for Patients

Please allow 2 weeks for delivery

Also available online at: www.Amazon.ca and www.Chapters.ca

You may order several copies in lots of 6 at 30% off.
For bulk or U.S. orders please contact rsb@meetyourheart.com or
fax your request to (705) 671-3147.

Further Resources For Priority Patients

A full version of the *Personal Health System* ™ diary is available for purchase as a unique portfolio designed to facilitate individual patient record keeping. Information regarding purchasing is located on the associated website.

The *Personal Health System* ™ website allows accurate record keeping by patients in an easy-to-use, flexible, electronic format. To view, visit www.personalhealthsystem.com

This website also links patients to The *Medical School For Patients* website which contains materials for further patient education. This website is currently free and may be viewed at www.medicalschoolforpatients.com.

Dr. Baigrie is also available to receive your comments and feedback or request for in-house group seminars on "Secrets of Becoming a Priority Patient". Contact the authors at RSB@meetyourheart.com or by fax at (705) 671-3147.

See reverse of this page for order form.